Unstoppable Goddess

Every Woman's Guide to Freedom, Fulfilment & Success

Anna Letitia Cook

www.womenup.global

DEDICATION

to Ben and Lucy

– the sun shines brightest around them!

CONTENTS

CONTENTS

ACKNOWLEDGEMENTS

The biggest thank you of all goes to my amazing children, Ben and Lucy, who instead of saying 'Oh God, Mum's off on one with this becoming an author,' were totally supportive of me in this venture.

To Rhonda and Julie for their unfailing support and willingness to listen and give constructive feedback on all my ideas.

To Selkie who, all those years ago, showed me what love and freedom really mean. Thank you for all the fun, adventure, warmth, laughter, generosity, loyalty – and, of course, the prawns!

Tremendous gratitude to the Experts: Mariela Dabbah, John Strelecky, Jo-Ann Hamilton and Ceri Wheeldon for their great generosity and support in sharing their expertise.

Many thanks to the talented businesswomen Louise O'Sullivan, Ruth Sacks, Stina Ehrensvard and Gabriele Zedlmayer who unstintingly gave their time and shared their experience.

To Ian Brodie and Steve Gordon whose positive encouragement motivated me to write this book.

To the extremely talented Josh Jaques, a wonderful designer whose ability to produce creative and artistic masterpieces – particularly from my confused babblings – is a pleasure to see.

Special thanks – and several bottles of wine – to Tricia Johnson, a very professional and highly respected journalist, for good-humouredly proofing and commenting on the whole manuscript.

INTRODUCTION

"There are many spokes on the wheel of life.
First, we're here to explore new possibilities."

- Ray Charles

This book is a call to freedom – freedom of choice. Women's equality and women in the workplace are controversial issues – so much so that women are under enormous pressure to perform without always considering what they really want. Whether or not we want a high-flying career – I see a lot of women pushed into, or out of, doing something because of their upbringing, peer pressure and general expectations – we have to arrive at a point where all women can choose for themselves what they want to do, and be appreciated and respected for their choice and their talent.

My clients are often professional and executive women who come to me for mentoring and coaching in order to align their ideal career choices and achieve freedom, fulfilment and leadership success. Equally, many are women who wish to change direction, do something different, become entrepreneurs and live more in line with their passions, their interests and according to their choices.

I have worked with too many who are stressed and frustrated. Sadly, the majority either know they aren't doing what they want but aren't sure what that is, or are being

3

blocked in career progress because they aren't getting the respect and appreciation they deserve from their peers and superiors – often 'bypassed or forgotten' in favour of their male colleagues when promotion is available.

These and other challenges faced by my women clients were the inspiration for my creation of the SCOPE process for career fulfilment and success.

What is SCOPE?

SCOPE (Scrutinise, choose/change, overcome/organise, plan, evolve) is a simple, step-by-step blueprint to help you find the personal and career fulfilment you want and deserve.

Many clients come to me feeling empty; not fully engaged in their work, frustrated by lack of career development, constrained by company policies, slow-acting hierarchy or overly traditional ways of looking at employee potential.

Often, my clients have realised that they aren't passionate about their work (or life), and feel there is more out there. However, they can't quite put their finger on where, what or how... SCOPE will help you find your passion and clarity and give you a step-by-step guide to realising the personal and career fulfilment you want.

What does SCOPE do for you?

It helps you get clear on what you want to be and do and how to choose which aspects you need to change in order to get that. You find what will fulfil you and how to organise the plan to transition from where you are now to where you want to be – enjoying your life and work. You will gain impressive insights on your thought processes, your actions and reactions, your real strengths and talents, where your interests really lie and ultimately, what you want to experience in your life and how to achieve it.

SCOPE will give you the opportunity to discover who you really are and who you are meant to be. You will learn how to be honest with yourself, and make your choices from that position of self-knowledge. This is the key to your freedom to choose.

Once you have made your choices, you will put into place the changes and organisation necessary to create and follow your strategic plan to achieve your objectives in your life and career, so you can enjoy the freedom and fulfilment you are looking for.

What does the SCOPE process consist of?

S – Scrutinise your predeterminations

The first step in this process is to scrutinise where we are affected by outside influences – be it childhood predeterminations, peer pressure or any other kind of intimidation or persuasion, conscious or unconscious, which distracts us from what are our own true values, beliefs, wishes, dreams and objectives.

As adults, we often find the outside influences come from our colleagues and superiors at work, our friends who may be fast-tracking and expect you to do the same, or our husband and/or family who may be unsupportive of your wishes and prefer to take you in a different direction. All this – as well as the stress, anxiety and guilt that we all too frequently place on ourselves due to the beliefs and opinions of other people – can push us very far from our own true nature and freedom of choice.

Pinpointing weak points – or unconscious, self-sabotaging reactions – helps create clarity and self-knowledge through a series of exercises and analysis. Finding out what thoughts we are having and what actions we are taking because of outside influences – and realising how we behave because of them – can be liberating in itself. Then, we can choose – or not – to make the changes that better suit our own true self.

C – Choose/change your direction

To choose or change your direction to create a more fulfilling future you first have to know what you really want to do, and where your main interests and passions lie. Sounds easy, doesn't it! This is where the previous work and exercises on finding your predeterminations come in.

In this part of the process we dig down and find out what really does light your fire. We uncover any deeply hidden strengths and passions which existed before they were drowned out and stifled by all those outside influences, and we bring them to the fore.

We look at what you are doing now, and what you have done in your life and career to date. We will find out which aspects of your life have given you the most pleasure and the most rewarding experiences. We filter through the non-positive parts – those that drained your energy or made your eyes glaze over just thinking about them – but keep and use that knowledge as an element to be aware of in the choice of changes to integrate in your strategy organisation.

By focusing on what feelings you gain in various areas of your life and career and how different environments energise you – including how you view yourself through the different levels of environment, behaviour, capability, beliefs and values, and personal and professional context identity – we find what you really want for yourself so you can then choose how to achieve it for maximum fulfilment.

O – Overcome objections/organise your strategy

Being aware of and understanding how to overcome objections – both those appearing subconsciously in yourself and from those around you – is an essential part of this process. On an-all-too-regular basis, we self-sabotage or lack confidence because of some reason which, once acknowledged, is greatly diminished and so becomes manageable. This helps us keep on track and allows us to set boundaries for any new enterprises, therefore vastly reducing stress and minimising risk.

This stage includes exercises such as Fears and Doubts realignment, Personal SWOT (strengths, weaknesses, opportunities, threats) and the Wheel of Life. Some areas may need just a little tweak; with others you will need to focus on them in more detail. Once your plan is ready for action, being aware of these areas helps achieve clarity in your choices and aids your steady progress towards your goals.

Now you have reached the stage to organise your strategy. You know what you want; you know what skills, strengths and opportunities you have. You have become aware of – and anticipated – weaknesses, doubts, threats and potential problems that could crop up.

Congratulations – once you reach this stage you have already completed a major part of this journey! You are now ready to organise the hows, wheres and whens of taking your life and career to a new level of fulfilment and success.

P – Plan your action

Part 4 in the process is where we become very practical ….we actually plan! Using some exercises such as the TOWS (external threats and opportunities, internal weaknesses and strengths) matrix, the 'Hedgehog concept' and the PEST (political, economic, socio-cultural and technological changes) analysis to help outline priorities and the most effective order in which to act, we create the timeline for the actions and objectives we want to achieve – whether it be career development, entrepreneurial concepts or personal dreams.

You will find out how to integrate what you already know and have, what is directly available in the immediate vicinity, what you need to add to the mixture and where/how you can do this.

E – Evolve to your choice of career, fulfilment and success

Start the evolution! Whether it is changing your career direction, climbing to the highest rung on the career ladder, branching out and setting up your own business, creating a new and exciting you as you grow older – you have done all the scrutinising, choosing, organising and planning, so now is the time to start living it.

Through inspiring techniques, exercises and ongoing assessment, you put the process into practice, evaluating your progress, aligning and adapting as necessary while progressing with confidence, energy and motivation. Harvest the seeds you are sowing, enjoying each step along the way. You start to feel the new-found pleasure of transforming your talents, honing your skills and developing your passions in your choice of career, fulfilment and success.

With this book I hope to give women the knowledge and tools necessary to understand their situation and their own wishes, empowering them to be able to put into place the strategy that leads them to achieve what they really want in their life and career.

Achieving this is already an excellent and attainable goal, but in doing so, we must not forget that age old wisdom – healthy in mind, healthy in body, healthy in spirit. Freedom, fulfilment and success come from overall well-being which, in turn, is a quality of the whole and requires true health in mind, body and spirit! Health, fitness and nutrition help create emotional wellbeing, thus forming an integral part of the whole.

"To keep the body in good health is a duty, otherwise we shall not be able to keep our mind strong and clear."
- Buddha

1 WHAT IS SUCCESS?

"True success, true happiness
lie in freedom and fulfilment."

\- Dada Vaswani

Success is freedom! Success is fulfilment!

Why? Because it is only when we are truly fulfilled that we are happy, energised, full of joie de vivre, serene and at peace with ourselves and the world in which we live.

When we are fulfilled we become strong, natural leaders; we encourage and inspire those around us. We emanate incredible energy; we have a positive aura that lifts the mood of those we connect with.

Our passion, our drive and our creativity allow us to focus our talents in the direction that resonates with us, optimising our assets and achieving maximum productivity and greatest results. Our light really does shine at its brightest when we are fulfilled.

So what is the importance of freedom in achieving fulfilment? And, how do we achieve this superior state?

Freedom is our own freedom of choice in what we think, what we do, what we create and how we choose to pursue our life. Freedom is knowing that we take decisions with true self-knowledge, that the values we respect are our own, that our actions are taken – and reactions are caused – with awareness. It is being totally – and sometimes brutally - honest with ourselves about who we are, what we are and why we do something.

Often we are unconsciously influenced by predeterminations and peer pressure. This is something that can derail our progress quite seriously as well as cause great stress. We can find ourselves frustrated and blocked as a result of not being sure of where our real passions lie, nor being clear about the direction we want to take. This is why it is essential to get clear on these issues before moving any further forward in our lives and careers.

When we have this knowledge of self, this attitude, this mental freedom, we live from a position of confidence and strength. It gives us great clarity and focus.

When we combine this with our dreams, our passions, our skills and our talents we can create our own opportunities and achieve fulfilment and success in the direction of our choice.

For the deepest fulfilment we need to welcome the value of the whole mind-body experience. When every aspect is in harmony and flow, the greatest success and happiness is obtained. Therefore, healthy mind, healthy body! Incorporating all areas – mental, physical and emotional – will give you the optimal results to achieve fulfilment and success.

This means if we include nutrition, exercise and mind-set as being integral parts of the whole, we have a far greater capacity for achieving our objectives of freedom and fulfilment. Just for the moment, start mulling these over in your head. How much focus do you put on the following as integral ingredients for your fulfilment and success?

Nutrition and healthy eating:

- **Avoid** fast food, junk, salt, sugar, pre-prepared, processed, salamis, pâtés, cold cuts, etc; animal fats, most meat and dairy...

- **Favour** natural fresh, organic fruit, vegetables, leaves, salads, seeds, some fish, minimal quantities of organically raised meat if you absolutely must.

Exercise and fitness:

- Regular **activity** of your choice that incorporates stretching/flexibility, strength training and cardio. My favourites are dancing, walking, Pilates, yoga, T'ai chi.

- **Get out** in the sun and fresh air every day – try a daily 30-minute walk outside (building up to longer spells over time), preferably in the countryside but failing that, in a local park or beside a canal.

Mindset, mental/emotional relaxation:

- **Meditate** – or if you are uncomfortable with the idea of this, just make a regular quiet time for yourself each day, when you disconnect from the unavoidable stresses and strains of daily life.

- **Avoid** letting yourself react negatively in stressful situations

- **Focus** on your achievements – the small ones as much as the large ones

- **Hold** positive thoughts, positive actions and what you get pleasure from foremost in your mind.

- **Enjoy** all the moments in the day – not always fixating on goals. To use a well-known but very accurate cliché: enjoy the journey, not just the destination!

So where are you now when you think of your success. Are you truly fulfilled? Are you halfway there, just starting or haven't even thought about this vision of success?

A good place to start is by discovering what fulfilment looks like to you. You can begin by doing this short, simple but very revealing exercise.

Exercise 1: Discovering fulfilment...

What do you like doing best?

Download the accompanying worksheet from http://unstoppablegoddess.life/book-resources/ or get a piece of paper and a pen.

So, what do you like doing best? What immediately springs to mind, both in your personal as well as your professional life?

*Think of what **you** like doing best – not your spouse, not your family or friends, not your colleagues ... just you. The others come later...*

Write down at least 20 ideas (or more...!)

Don't restrict yourself in any direction. ☺

Then write down what it is about these ideas that you like doing. How does it make you feel? What emotion can you associate with the idea?

To finish up this first stage, circle any that have recurring feel-good factors associated with the ideas; any that feature the same recurring emotions.

Underline the top three emotions and keep coming back to them over the next week.

In all you do on a daily basis, just note to yourself when you feel these top three emotions and what you are doing at the time.

"People take different roads seeking fulfilment and happiness. Just because they're not on your road doesn't mean they've gotten lost."

- H. Jackson Brown, Jr.

I would like to introduce you to Louise. She is a wonderful example of the ethos of this book because she is an excellent businesswoman, proud mother of four, CEO of a successful company and has won numerous business awards. Louise inspires me not only for these great attributes, but also for her passion for life, her energy, her independence and free choice in her actions, together with the obvious fulfilment she has found in her life and career. Louise very generously gave her time and shared her experience and views on what it takes to really achieve freedom, fulfilment and success as a woman in today's world...

 . **Experience Talks:**

Finding Career Fulfilment

A conversation with Louise O'Sullivan

Former CEO of ANAM Technologies, recipient of the '50 Most Inspiring Women in European Tech' award, Advocate for gender parity in the IT Industry and Strategic Advisor at #techmums

What is the first thing that comes to mind when you hear about women's freedom to choose what they really want to do?

That it doesn't exist for the majority of women today because we are not taught to either know it or want it!

List three pieces of advice on obtaining career fulfilment.

Know that it is not selfish to be ambitious and want a successful career

Don't feel you have to choose between motherhood or career – you can have both and we should work hard to ensure all women should be able to make this choice

Don't allow any judgement of you according to today's social norms get in the way of your ambition

What are three mistakes people commonly make about career objectives?

Not recognising that every experience is enormously valuable, and that experience of failure is a key part of success. As women, we tend to shy away from the risk of failure or rejection – which is shying away from some valuable experiences. Chalk everything down to experience; pick yourself up and get going again

Believing you are not capable of the job and that someone is going to find you out. You have to back yourself, because when you do, others do. Also recognise that doing enough well is better than not doing anything in case it isn't perfect.

That once you have your children you are on the career shelf and a less valuable member of your career industry than before motherhood. This is one of the greatest myths of all time and one which women would do well to bust. Industries would do well to get over it too, because they would benefit from a massive untapped and valuable labour force.

What are some actionable takeaways you would like to leave women about change and choosing what is right for them?

We live in an incredible era of change for women and it is a privilege to be part of seeing this change happen. We are a long way from the Utopia I would like to see for my children but the process is in play. All of us have a part to play in making a change for future generations. Different people have different causes in life – for some it is environment, for some it's politics and others, poverty. All these things need to see change and for me, it is women's freedom to choose and be independent in their own right that is so important.

I was born at the tail end of an era where female subservience had presided for millennia, based on the constraints of female reproduction. This belief has been embedded in all cultures – but it is currently undergoing a seismic change that began in the last century.

With the advancements that have occurred in the last 100 years – scientifically, medically, educationally and politically – women have now been provided with options. It is because of these options that choices we make will affect and benefit the next generation.

For example, if you have the choice and the means to recycle your recyclables, why would you not do it if you know it will have a positive effect on the environment for the next generation? In the same way, if you have the choice and the means to make a difference for the freedoms of the next generation of women, why would you not act?

Why is career fulfilment important?

When George Mallory was asked by a reporter in 1924 why he wanted to climb Everest, his immortal response was: '*Because it is there.*'

Historically, we women have been taught that our fulfilment comes exclusively from being a good wife, having children, being a good mother and keeping a good home for our husband who controls our financial and social future.

We have educated our daughters – who are often higher academic achievers than our sons – but then ripped apart their ambitions to attain the highest possible accolades, because of the pressure of these age-old expectations. We have believed that women cannot have both.

Career fulfilment is just that. Fulfilment. For most women, career is a compromise and that is because the career culture only allows for the phase of fatherhood, not motherhood.

So why is it important that women should attain career fulfilment??

Because this is our 'Everest'. We live in an age of medical, educational and technical advancement, meaning that not only will we survive our childbearing years, but we may also postpone having our children for longer, and be healthier and have more energy and options than previous generations.

We need to pioneer and explore our fulfilment – from leaving school through to retirement. We need to learn how to embrace our personal ambition and know we are allowed to do so without being judged or put in a box. We always talk about wanting our children to be happy, but unless we set the example for our daughters, they will not know how to achieve it. In fulfilment we find happiness. Don't we all have a right to that?

2 PREDETERMINATIONS AND PEER PRESSURE... HOW THEY MAKE YOU ACT

We would expect professional women (and men) to already have the skills and experience to define what they really want and achieve it – particularly if they have gone through extensive skills and strategy training while at university and business schools. Sadly, analysing one's own goals is rarely dwelt on. Everything is focused on the company – the business strategy, the results to be obtained for the employer or organisation – and we forget about ourselves.

Knowing what you want to do

Some of us do know exactly what we want but there are far more of us who don't. Many people enter the job market each year. With the pressure of a large influx of candidates competing for the number of positions available, and the mundane necessity of having to pay the bills, we often start by doing more or less whatever is available.

As you progress further in your career, you get promotion and other opportunities, but you do tend to stay very much on the track that you originally started – and this can clear away any thoughts of what you really want or what your dream job or career might be.

Do we realise we are doing something we don't actually want to do?

This leads us towards the effect of predeterminations on our life and career. We frequently choose our path because of family pressure or unconsciously, because we're following the expectations with which we grew up.

For example, quite often if you have a very high-flying mother as a career model – which I know currently is more unusual – you'll probably feel the expectation to do something similar. Equally, your mother might provide a totally opposite example, as it was in my case.

My mother was a very capable woman and served on many committees, but strongly believed a woman's proper position was as a housewife looking after her children and her husband. She found it very shocking that married women and mothers wanted a career.

She regularly told me that a woman's priority was to stay at home with husband and children. I didn't agree with this – but nevertheless I found it very difficult not to subconsciously react to her criteria for "success" which were being the perfect mother, housewife and hostess.

A lot of this is caused by predeterminations. Predeterminations are when the way in which we do something is influenced by the way we've been brought up, but we're not usually aware that this is the case.

Mariela Dabbah, award-winning author and international speaker on issues related to education, career development and success, explains this in more detail in her interview at the end of this chapter, but for the moment I will give a few examples.

Predeterminations and peer pressure

If a father has been a financial wizard, quite often you'll find the son will try to follow in his footsteps, or the family will expect the son to go into the same area of work when perhaps deep down, the child wants to do something completely different.

For example, I know a family where the father was one of the top stockbrokers in Europe. His son went to university and studied economics – when his passion was cooking and all he really wanted was to be a chef.

He had grown up in an environment where only glittering careers in business and high finance were really appreciated. I know that from the parents' point of view, the positioning and influence were unconscious, but that's the way they were thinking and so for the son, it was natural to follow into the same area.

You get the same thing in many professions – particularly among doctors, lawyers, the armed services, farmers and so on, because it's what families respect and believe is a good thing to do. And this is not just because of any kudos these professions may hold, but also because they allow you to help people and give to the community.

Often you'll find the parents, family and friends will do everything possible to help the child follow into 'their' profession when it's not what the child wants at all.

Once you have entered the workforce you see a similar response from colleagues – peer pressure – about the job, field or sector you are in. You may have great talent in one particular area, but you are not encouraged to shine in this direction because it doesn't quite fit the mould!

Quite often it can be like this for people in sales – undoubtedly because sales skills equal good financial results for the company. The person is excellent at their job but it's not really what they like – however because they're good at it, they receive encouragement and opportunities from the boss and colleagues alike. In fact, the person would much rather work in an area more in line with their passions and interests.

We're influenced by everything around us without being aware of it. Rarely do we think to actually look at what these predeterminations are, or where the peer pressure comes from. And quite often we follow through in this uninspiring direction automatically.

Effect of predeterminations – are they always bad or negative?

Predeterminations are not always bad, but in general, they are a bad influence if they result in you doing something that is really different to what your inner character wants to do, or is contrary to your natural feelings or instincts.

If you're in this situation, you can be very unhappy – but you may not be consciously aware of the reasons behind the way you feel. You may just have a feeling of dissatisfaction, of not being really comfortable with your work, of finding things stressful or of not having energy and/or passion.

You're not necessarily UNhappy – but you're just not happy and energised.

This, in its extreme, can lead to stress which obviously doesn't help you find freedom, fulfilment or success. There are so many problems relating to stress, leading to depression, irritability, bad relationships etc. It can spill over into your personal life just as much as your professional one.

However, some predeterminations are quite constructive.

For example, if your family has always worked hard, been dedicated, loyal and paid attention to detail, these attributes can really be helpful for you in your work environment or professional career, because you automatically follow suit.

Again, if your family is very caring, and think it's important to help people try and support the local community, this can also be very positive for you – both on a professional and a personal basis.

If you have a family that strongly believes you have the right to an opinion, the right to ask yourself what you want to do and the right to contribute to discussions, this can be extremely positive because it can help you to become more open-minded and an excellent leader.

To my mind, an ideal positive predetermination would be where your family is supportive and from when you were young, has asked you for your opinion – what you thought, whether you liked something and encouraged you to take a stand...

That gives you confidence. It also encourages you to analyse what happens around you so you have a more objective and more lucid view of the world.

The following exercise can remind you of your childhood dreams and interests, and make you aware of where parental and family influences may have impacted your decisions.

Exercise 2: Sourcing Fulfilment

What are your dreams?

Download the accompanying worksheet from http://unstoppablegoddess.life/book-resources/ or get a piece of paper and a pen.

When you were a child, what dreams did you have? What did you want to be when you grew up? What games did you choose to play during your playtime? (This last question applies to when you had totally free choice, and not when you were being influenced by someone else.)

It doesn't matter how far-fetched your dreams and aspirations were. Childhood dreams don't have any restrictions – your imagination flew in any direction and this is so very liberating! ☺

Then write down why you wanted to do these things. What was the dream associated with them, and how did it make you feel?

Now look for predeterminations. Think of the reactions of your parents and family to your imagination and your dreams. Were all your childhood choices your own free choices, or were they unconsciously stimulated by your parents' approbation or disapproval?

Often we don't realise how much we do things because of outside influences. It isn't wrong, but we need to be aware of the origins of our ideas and aspirations. Try and clarify which were your own, without any stimuli from others, and which were influenced. Over the next week, mull these over and note down any more that pop into your head. Whenever you have a quiet moment, you can think about this and about how you felt when you imagined yourself becoming what you wanted to be, or doing what you wanted to do.

To finish up this stage, circle the dreams and games that have the strongest feel-good factors associated with them – and any that generate the same recurring emotions.

Underline the top three emotions and keep coming back to the ideas and emotions over the next week.

In all you do on a daily basis, just note to yourself when you feel these emotions and what you are doing at the time.

Peer pressure influence – what is it?

Peer pressure influence is very much alive in the workplace. It can start in university with your fellow students, and then continue on with your colleagues, your managers, your directors – whatever level you're at – who expect you to follow a certain route.

For example, you could start off as an Assistant Manager. Then, two different opportunities come up: you could be promoted to become a Senior Manager, or there could be an opportunity to move laterally to another department, without a promotion.

Peer pressure comes if your colleagues expect you to go for the higher level promotion, without taking into account that it might not be exactly what you want.

Peer pressure can be very positive and supportive – but it can also be negative and block a lot of opportunities, as well as make you feel uncomfortable or rejected if you don't follow others' expectations.

At its worst, it can cause some of us to be totally dominated – particularly when we're not aware ourselves of the choices or why we're making them. So, inside we might not be happy with the idea of senior management, but we're not aware of it. We might naturally be much more creative by nature and want to go in a different direction.

If we are dominated by the influence and opinions of others, and predeterminations from the way that we've grown up, it can strongly affect the way we work, the way we channel our career in the company and our choices regarding moving to the next level.

This can be the same when working in – or leading – a team. We take on more responsibility; we do the extra projects or assignments – and sometimes it can become very overpowering. This extra responsibility does not always place us in situations that let us shine; it doesn't use all of our strengths and it doesn't let our creativity and natural talent flow through. But because everyone expects us to do it, we battle on because we don't want to feel we have let them down – or we don't want them to think badly of us.

If we don't freely choose and have a genuine passion for what we are doing, we can end up almost shutting down – becoming like a robot. Even though we might be very competent, emotionally we no longer have any passion for the job.

Recognising the signs that you aren't following your own path

Probably the most obvious sign that we aren't following a path that we have freely chosen is when we feel a lack of passion – a lack of curiosity. We feel tired; perhaps we don't have as much energy as we used to. Even our curiosity for anything connected to a specific project – or our work in general – seems to disappear.

We lose motivation when we aren't following our own choices. We might be super-organised in our way of doing something – ticking off on a list, "Okay I've done that, I've done that." But the inspiration to create, to think outside the box, to find other solutions dies. We don't still have the spark of, "What if I added this? What if I did that?"

The above are examples of peer pressure for women in their careers. It is just as active for women staying at home with children.

Career or stay-at-home mum. How do we know if we are reacting to peer pressure rather than our own choice?

If you have any of these symptoms at work, and if you either have or want children, consider seriously if you feel obliged to go to work or push yourself to have a 'good' career when in fact you really want to be at home bringing up your children, spending time with them and being fully present in their lives.

With today's fights facing women, such as women's equality, gender balance, parity – however you wish to phrase it – it can be easy to be swept along with the tide and end up committing ourselves to a career when in fact with the birth of our children, we realise that the magnificent career we had always dreamed of is really not the priority we had previously imagined. We can become hemmed in by our own career success and it can be very difficult to change the focus gracefully – so much so that some of us give up and continue going to work and moving up that ladder, when a large, well-hidden part of our heart is bleeding and tormented because of the deep, overwhelming – and often unforeseen – desire to be immersed in our children and the great pleasure and fulfilment of being a mother.

For those who have chosen the experience of staying at home as a mother and housewife, we have the same clues about whether we really are choosing for ourselves or not. If you stay at home with the children, it can be because you think you want to be with them, but in fact you're frustrated. Or, again, you might feel permanently tired and are constantly irritable – and not just because of a temporary reaction to a problem or a few bad nights' sleep.

If you don't seem to be able to maintain your normal good humour, or if your moods are very up and down, it could be because you're staying at home when really, you would like to have children but also keep your career.

How can you become aware of these issues relating specifically to yourself?

You might feel slightly sad; slightly frustrated. You need to look at what you're doing in the workplace and what you were doing before, and think about what you wanted when you were younger. Also consider where you see yourself in four or five years' time.

Then with that, look at the family around you; look at the idea of having a child and think about all the stages of it – really try to visualise it.

If you feel happy and energised, that's great. If you feel, "Yes I'd love to do this for two or three years and then I'd like to go back to work and do X, Y and Z," then you know that you've actually made the choice that you want to make – for you.

If you're unsure, or thinking, 'Well yes I **should** do this," bear in mind that many times when we're doing something we don't want to do, we say, "I should." This is a sign that we are feeling the pressure of what somebody else wants, and not really what we want. If you want it, you would say, "I want to do this," instead of, "I should do this."

How do we know if we're lying to ourselves?

Normally when we have that hollow feeling inside it's a sign that we are lying to ourselves. Or, when you say, "I want to do this, I want to do that," and you have a whole lot of things that you say you're passionate about - but you never do them and they never happen.

When you focus on all the problems in doing something, you're very slow to get it done or you feel tired, these are all signs that you're lying to yourself.

When you are really passionate about something, you don't even notice the time. You don't see the problems.

When you're lying to yourself, you think, "Okay, my parents would like this, my husband would like that, my boss would like that." You might say to yourself, "I'd really like to be a company director," or, "I think it would be fantastic to do x and I can always do y ... blah, blah, blah". But when it comes down to actually making the move, you're not very dynamic. You're always finding problems that you have to overcome first – basically, you're procrastinating. Often when we do this, it's actually because we're lying to ourselves about wanting to do whatever it is.

Can you change predeterminations or the pressure from others? If so, how?

Yes, you can. With the exercise that we did earlier, which already helps you think more about what you heard when you grew up and what you hear around you at work. Changing predeterminations can be as simple as actually realising which ones are in your thoughts and reactions. I'll give myself as an example: When I was first married to a director, it was normal that I hosted a lot of dinners with other directors and their wives, building the social network and being the proper company wife.

I used to go to a huge amount of trouble with these dinners, and I would take ages to organise them. However, I used to avoid asking people too often and basically, quite often I looked for excuses.

Now I can see that it was because deep down, I didn't want to do it but at the time, I wasn't aware of this.

Now if I'm in that sort of situation, or have any sort of career situation to make, I think, "Okay, do I really want to do this? Or is it something that is 'expected' of me? Is my reaction to it left over from when I was younger?" And as soon as I know the answers to these questions, I'm quite happy. I can feel my mood getting better.

If you feel passionately full of energy and can't wait to start doing whatever it is, and you push away anything blocking it, then it's pretty obvious that it really is what you want.

Just knowing that something is a predetermination gives you power. It means you can then decide, "Okay, either I will do it or I won't." You have the freedom to choose.

Sometimes, just knowing that you've recognised it as a predetermination gives you as much power as you need, so you feel okay. You feel you can channel your energy because you've accepted that you've chosen to do whatever it is, instead of being forced into it.

So how can you make your own choices?

If you think about what you're trying to do and you feel that you're being obliged to do it, you need to consider the consequences of not doing it. Then decide whether the consequence of not doing it will be too unpleasant for you or for somebody else. Next, you prioritise. Do an analysis of the consequences. This sounds like it takes a long time but in fact, you do it in a fraction of a second. For the more serious things in your life and their ramifications, you may ask the question, "Do you need to think about it more deeply?"

It just gives you the opportunity of deciding, "Does this fit in with what I really want to do, or does it go against it? Will the reaction of people around me be too negative? Do I care about it? Will I enjoy doing it or not?" And then you make the choice.

You might decide, "Okay I don't want to do it but I don't want to hurt somebody so I'll do part of it." It doesn't have to be black or white – you can have your own shades of grey within it. The important thing is you now have the freedom to make your own free choice.

What happens if it feels – or seems – like rejection of family and friends?

Often, with situations like this, we think we're rejecting our family and friends. This is partly because we're feeling guilty about taking over our own independence. We've grown up always being told, "You must think about other people; you must do this for somebody else," and we get programmed to do it.

Think about those around you. Often they just say, "No, I can't do it because of X, Y or Z." We accept it happily; we don't expect them to do everything. But we tend to put ourselves under pressure to do far more – to be Superwoman, capable of absolutely everything.

Sometimes with our peer pressure and our predeterminations, we need to just step out of the picture and think about it more objectively. Rejection isn't the same as having a different opinion or a different belief.

I totally disagree with what some of my best friends think about an issue or with their values – not because they're bad, but their opinions just aren't the same as mine. It isn't rejection – I still love my friends and I still love my family, but they don't always think the same way as I do on a particular subject and I respect that.

You can frequently find that thinking and behaving differently can be more enriching for you, your relationship and the whole environment in which you live.

How do you avoid hurting family and friends?

If you're doing something – or if you choose something – which you know is really against what they believe, and if they are likely to react badly, it is best to progress gently and with compassion, respecting their beliefs and values. Don't be harsh or aggressive in the way you broach the subject.

Explain in a discreet and non-confrontational way that you just want to try something different – a little compromise could be in order. Maybe it's not 100 per cent going with what you believe, or what your choice is, but sometimes we do need to think of others and avoid unnecessary and hurtful conflict.

Using freedom of choice to act or not to act

Once you've understood what your predeterminations are, and what is almost pre-programmed behaviour and reaction, it gives you a lot of freedom in your head. Why? Because you know what you are doing now, and you know what you have been doing previously. You understand that your reactions stem from the way you've been brought up, the habits that you've fallen into or the expectations of the workplace.

This gives you the freedom of choice to decide if you want to continue in that way or not.

Sometimes you can just accept that it's not what you really want, but you don't have a problem with doing it. The fact that you know you want to do something else gives you your own personal inner sense of freedom. You don't always have to show it externally.

If you decide you do want to act, then start putting in place the method of doing it. One step at a time, start planning out what you really want to do.

May I introduce you to Mariela. She is the shining light who first inspired me on my quest for women's equality – particularly in the workplace. She opened my eyes to how difficult it can be to get the respect and appreciation you deserve, and to understand the different skills and approach necessary so you can be seen – and treated – as an equal both as a colleague and a leader in today's world.

 ## ASK the EXPERT:

Mariela Dabbah - Award-winning author, founder and CEO of Red Shoe Movement, international speaker on issues related to education, career development and success

What is the first thing that comes to mind when you hear about women's freedom to choose what they really want to do?

It's still such a difficult topic for women. Regardless of where they live – even for women in the most developed countries – exercising the freedom to choose what they want for themselves is hard. Some have never given it much thought at all; they just go through the motions and fulfil all or most of the roles society or their families expect of them.

Can you briefly explain what are mandates, messages received and predeterminations?

As a newborn, you as a person are undetermined because you still haven't created your own identity. This primal need to find comfort in another human to affirm that we exist begins at birth. You may be aware that babies need to connect with their mother's body, warmth, pulse and gaze. They need to be touched, cuddled and rocked in order to develop abilities such as empathy. Well, that initial recognition from others to endorse your existence carries certain predeterminations. In psychology, these are defined as the concepts and ideas that precede any conscious decision by the individual. Think about the ancestral, genetic and societal influences that have nothing to do with a person's own will. They are instilled into children very early on – such things as what your parents and grandparents dream for you, the expectations they had for you from when you were in your mother's womb and so on. It's through the process of detaching yourself from these predeterminations that you become a person.

These predeterminations, or subconscious mandates, come in the way of verbal and non-verbal messages that we carry through our lives without being aware of them. For example, if in your country – or in your family – women are always expected to be the ones in charge of the household, regardless of whether or not they work outside the home, you can have a hard time asking your husband for help with dinner because you have a meeting. You feel guilty and find ways to juggle everything and this ends up stressing you out. Or you pass on opportunities for career growth that involve travelling because you wouldn't be around to supervise the household. That's how predeterminations affect your behaviour and your career opportunities.

What are three mistakes people make due to these?

First: They allow their subconscious mandates to keep them in a place where they don't want to be. If you grew up believing men are the ones making all the financial decisions and you have a hard time negotiating your promotions or salary with your male boss, it's time to revisit those old ideas.

Second: They assume their circumstances are much more fixed than they are and feel powerless to change them. For most of us, our predeterminations are a soundtrack we don't even recognise as being separate from us. We think, "This is who I am" and, "This is what is expected of me" are unchangeable ideas. They are not. Many of them have been part of our lives since before we can remember and so we are familiar with them. That doesn't mean we can't change them and create new declarations of who we are – and who we want to become.

Third: They disregard the effect of subconscious mandates on others. Male executives who don't acknowledge that women have different mandates to men run the risk of alienating their employees. So rather than creating an environment suitable for growth and engagement, they inadvertently turn women employees off. If you are a male executive and you understand that women may have a harder time taking a risk – because they'd like to feel they are 100 per cent ready before they accept a stretch assignment – coach them. Encourage them to take the risk – even if they are only 60 per cent ready. Avoid the easy path of not even offering the opportunity to women, presuming they will turn you down.

What are some actionable takeaways you would like to leave women about overcoming these hurdles, making the changes and choosing what is right for them?

Become aware of the old verbal and non-verbal messages related to gender roles which you carry from before you were born and while you were growing up. Evaluate their usefulness for your current and future career goals and overall happiness. If they don't agree with where you'd like to go next, or with what you'd love your life to be like, replace them with more powerful declarations that are better aligned with those goals. (Read my book, 'Find your Inner Red Shoes', for exercises to help you with this.)

Why is career fulfilment important?

Research shows that the more engaged and happy you are at work, the happier you are with your life in general. And the way to feel happier is to feel in control of your decisions and your career. Are you doing what you really love? Is your value recognised and appreciated? Is your professional activity in alignment with your life goals? These are the questions you should be asking yourself.

You can find Mariela at www.RedShoeMovement.com and RedShoeMovement and MarielaDabbah across social media.

3 SELF-DISCOVERY,
WHAT DO YOU REALLY WANT?

It's important to know what you really want to do and what your passions are, because when you don't know, you end up going round and round in circles. You change jobs, you don't feel comfortable, you try a lot of different thing and then you look back thinking, "I failed. I haven't done anything. I'm no good. I can't do it." You try too many things and because your passion isn't there, you don't ever fully commit to anything.

How deeply do you need to go into self-discovery for this to help?

I am asked this question oh, so many times! The simple answer is that you need to go into it very deeply. Even approaching it in a shallow way is going to help to a degree, but ideally, go right down to the absolute depths of your interior and find out exactly what you want.

When you do that, it's almost like a well-oiled machine – everything works and everything falls into place.

The more you know about what you want, the more you have the opportunity of aligning where you are now with where you want to go – but also understanding who you are, and knowing your own values and beliefs.

It gives you confidence. It's like reassurance – you just feel more energised; you feel happier in yourself because you know yourself. You can treat yourself as a friend.

The impact on your life and career

Once you know, it gives you a real freedom. It gives you an incredible energy because you go in the right direction – the direction that suits you.

When you think of someone who is absolutely passionate about what they do, you want to be with them. They make you feel alive because their whole fibre is completely committed and involved in what they do.

If you think of what you're doing now – maybe at work – perhaps you're enjoying it. If you are, that's great. But maybe there are times when you just sit there thinking, "Oh God, when can I go home?" Just consider, which answer is better for you?

If you are doing something that you're totally passionate about – so much so that you don't even notice the time – you get things done two, three, four times faster because everything is flowing. All of yourself is pumping along. Your brain is working, your ideas are coming and so are your organisational skills.

It's like being an athlete: everything is at its maximum and you're doing your absolute best. This is a great situation – this is your ideal life situation. When you are happy, you're much more interested in your life. It makes you more focused, yet more relaxed. It increases the energy which you put towards your work, your career, your relationships, your life. It improves everything.

Finding out what you really want

If you don't know, the best thing you can do to start with is analyse what you wanted when you were younger – that always helps. Then think about what you are good at, and about your strong points.

Going back to basics and jotting down a lot of different possibilities will really help you achieve clarity.

The effect of family, and fitting what you truly want into the family environment

Once you have discovered what you really want, your whole situation and path through life become so much easier. You know whether you want to have a family; you can decide in what environment you would like to bring up your children; you can integrate your choices regarding career and future responsibilities in a way that interests you, and you will know which direction you need to take in order to achieve this.

Armed with this knowledge, you will find it so much easier to align your dreams to fit in with someone else's, and negotiate acceptable levels of compromise. Often, we find that "family" consumes a large amount of time in our life – which is wonderful unless you don't really want it to; it's very good to find this out in advance!

Anything to which you have to commit a large part of your life can be difficult if you don't like or enjoy it. If you know what you like and enjoy, it makes good relationships easier – particularly with your husband and your children. You can integrate your family life to make it more enriching, and have more possibilities and opportunities which give you a stronger relationship with your family members. It makes you a much more generous and supportive mother because your whole outlook and emotions are so much more positive and productive.

What is the effect of this knowledge on career progress and ultimate success?

Once you have your knowledge, you can channel yourself and your energy properly. If you're at a certain stage in your career and getting frustrated – perhaps you want promotion – knowing your inner strengths, passions, objectives and requirements for fulfilment can give you the edge when you're up against people in the workplace who are as good as you; there is a lot of competition out there. Challenging this from a position of self-knowledge and confidence is a far more comfortable – as well as successful – experience.

When you know what you're really meant to do and you're really happy doing it, you can be far more focused in your career and go for the ultimate. You can plan how, what, where and when – and thus you can prioritise. Anyone who's working with you senses the energy. They sense the creativity; they sense your positivity.

It's like having a special magic power – you have a different aura at work. You attract the right people to you and you remain happier and more capable. Any problems that arise are easier to deal with, and solutions are quicker to find.

You have an added confidence; you have an added level of focus and that is obviously going to come to the attention of your superiors. If you are already at a very high level, it makes your results much better – more inspired. It lets you help the company to progress at a faster rate and it makes you a much more supportive leader for your team.

Unfortunately, many women believe that being able to do what they want is only a dream and not a practical option. Unless you are talking about extremes – like being the first woman to land on Mars (or Venus!) – the vast majority of what we want is possible to a greater or lesser extent, depending on our own choice, our own decisions and our own commitment to ourselves. Something can be a dream and difficult to put in place, but often when you think that, it's actually because you're still lying to yourself and you haven't really cut through all the predeterminations. You haven't learned how to be totally clear with yourself, and you haven't discovered your true passions. In these cases, I would say you need to think in more depth about what you really want, and you need to do more work on whether you're being totally clear and frank with yourself.

This exercise may help you…

Exercise 3: Exploring how associating your imagination with your identity, values and beliefs can pave the way for clarity, focus and fulfilment...

You can download the accompanying worksheet from the resources section http://unstoppablegoddess.life/book-resources/ or get a piece of paper and a pen.

What are your favourite books and films of all time? Choose two or three of each.

With which character(s) do you feel an affinity? Which characters do you dislike?

Write down the name of the book/film, what you like about the story and which identity and emotions it touches in you.

What is the power in the story that draws you to it?

Now think about the behaviour and actions of the hero/heroine you relate to the most. What do you like about them and why? How do they make you feel? What reaction do you have? Does this reaction make you happy, sad? Do you empathise? Does it inspire you to courage, action, generosity? (Often who and what we like in books and films link with our values of how we would like to be, act or do more of in our own lives.)

Out of all that you have written down, choose the main idea that you relate to most from the book/film and underline it, then circle the top three values and emotions that you relate to in the characters.

Recap:

*Let this percolate in your head **for three or four days** and then come back to do a recap of what you have discovered from these first three exercises.*

Now, write a clearer, more condensed list of the main points you have highlighted from your recap. Next to them, give examples of what you are currently doing in your life that involves any of these.

NB. Download the worksheet that goes with this exercise and other resources here...
http://unstoppablegoddess.life/book-resources/

You can start with small steps. You don't have to have the great big goal at the end right now. You need to enjoy what you're doing – but you also need to enjoy getting there.

Many people focus on having a new job, new responsibility or a new something-or-other as a goal. They focus so much on this goal that they forget there's a long journey involved in getting there. When they actually get the goal, what's left? There's nothing left; they've got there and there's nothing left to do.

With your dream, you need to think about what is close to it now. Think about the little steps that you're going to take in order to get there and put one small step in place at a time.

You need to differentiate between real dreams and idle fantasies. Put down on paper why you want your dream. Start thinking about the emotions – the reasoning behind it.

For example, I often say, "Okay, when I'm at the top of the Himalayas, I'm going to feel complete freedom." Now is this because I really want that? Or is it because I'm running away from something else?

.So I need to sync with the dream: "What feeling is it going to give me? Is it a conquest? Is it an inner peace? Is it serenity?" You need to know why you want this goal/dream – it may be just that – a dream – but you have to have some kind of tangible emotion that goes with it.

What you wanted to be as a child can have a strong relation to fulfilment in your adult life and job satisfaction. When you're a child, your imagination is boundless. There isn't as much influence from other people trying to make you do something. Your childhood imagination is coming from the inside – without you actually thinking about what can stop it happening; what the problems could be etc, etc.

When you think about your childhood dreams and what you wanted to do as a child, if you can find some kind of link between these and your adult life, it will really help you with fulfilment and satisfaction. What you wanted when you were little was natural to you; it was your innermost dreams, your innermost feelings – it made you feel good. It was only afterwards that you started to see boundaries. If you can recapture a little of your childhood in your adult life and your job, this leads to much more natural satisfaction.

How do you incorporate this into job satisfaction and workplace promotion?

When you feel good doing something, it is obvious by the way you react. You have more energy, more confidence and more power in yourself. You project the answers better; you project the action better. You allocate your team's responsibilities more suitably – all this makes your team feel more committed.

For example, think of someone who really enjoys travel. If you're working in an international company, you might find the opportunity to have that person work on a project that's dealing with expansion into another country. They will suddenly get so much more energy and so much more focus because it links to something that they really like. However, if they are assigned to the accounting side of doing statistics, for example, their energy dies and they stagnate.

A great management and leadership skill is finding out more options for the type of work someone might be best at. I think the person who best shows us the way to do is John Strelecky, in his book "*The Big Five for Life*". I have invited him to 'Ask the Expert' for this subject so you can hear his views and experiences later in the chapter.

Applying what you have learned:

Having done these exercises, the best way to apply them to life and career is to do it one step at a time. Don't feel that you have to do a big change immediately; you can start with small adjustments. For example, if what you really want to do is to work in the humanitarian sector in Latin America

– which would seem a difficult transition if you are actually employed in an office job in the UK – start by trying to help someone over there; you can become a sponsor or get involved with a Latin American company. Maybe mentor someone there by trying to help them understand more about business or your own field of work. You don't have to take an enormous, dramatic action straightaway.

Start by doing something that's easily accessible to you in your own environment – but which gets you closer to what you want to do. You'll get great satisfaction knowing that you're doing something more closely linked with who you really are. You don't have to reach the moon on Day One!

What is needed in order to change successfully?

Your mentality. You need to understand who you are and what you want; you need to accept that a certain modification to what you're doing will make you feel much better. You can continue getting a little closer, one step at a time. Many little steps over time make up a big distance and bring you nearer to your dream. And the essentials along every moment of the way? Enjoy the journey and focus on the present!

Incorporating this without too much effort – particularly when it seems different to current daily responsibilities – can seem challenging: a distinct move out of your comfort zone. This is the advantage of taking many little steps – it is easier to do and we feel so pleased to have done it. Therefore, pushing a little more and a little further soon becomes a new and pleasurable habit. Think about what you're doing at the moment and choose one little thing you could change in your life right now. Incorporate one new pleasurable item while at the same time, remove two of the more negative tasks. This is a very positive move – win-win in fact!

It could even be something really simple to begin with. For example, if timing is a problem, reorganise – change when you go shopping or to the gym. Change your working hours or what you usually do during your lunch hour or after work. Just reorganise slightly to give yourself a window to start incorporating this first step into your new and better life. Re-read your notes from the exercises about ideal vision etc, as this helps a great deal with motivation. You need to understand your identity, values and beliefs as they can be the key to you opening or closing doors for yourself.

So to summarise ...

It's important to have a clear vision in your head. Then create a strategy of what you want to do and why. Prioritise what to do and when to do it. Factor in what adjustments you might need to make with your current situation and your family. Then think about the little steps you need to start taking. And now, put it into action!

I am delighted to introduce you to John. With his Big Five for Life concept he truly shows us the importance of finding our meaning for life. He is the most inspiring person I know on the subjects of leadership and the best type of good business management to combine maximum employee fulfilment with optimal employer-employee relationships and respect. John advocates a true win-win vision for life, career, business and the whole workplace experience.

 ASK the EXPERT:

John P Strelecky - #1 bestselling author and inspirational speaker ("Big Five for Life" and the "Why Café" books, translated in over twenty-five languages, sold in over 40 countries, inspiring millions around the world). One of the Top 100 Thought Leaders in the field of leadership and personal development

What is the first thing that comes to mind when you hear about women's freedom to choose what they really want to do?

It wasn't that long ago that so many basic rights weren't available for women, such as the chance to work in a career of their choosing, to vote, to hold political office, to get a loan and so on. The women who struggled to secure those rights often gave up everything – including, in many cases, their lives. So one of the first things I think of is "obligation". That may seem like an odd word to have come to mind, but I think each woman today has an obligation to honour what so many others gave up, so that they could be free to choose. And the best way to fulfil that obligation is to live a free life. Courageously choose the existence you want to have, then courageously live that existence to the fullest extent of your capabilities.

When women do that, three wonderful events occur. First of all, they live an amazing life. Second, they honour those who sacrificed in order to help make it possible. And third, by living an authentic existence, they inspire those around them that they, too, can do the same.

What inspired you personally to choose to strike out and create your own future of success and fulfilment by following your 'Big 5 for Life'?

In my first book, The Why Cafe, I describe an experience on a beach in Costa Rica. The story is told through the words and experiences of one of the characters. It was my actual experience, though. I had been working since I was twelve years old; always pushing, always trying to get far enough ahead in life that I could finally take a breather and be free for a little while. When I was twenty-eight, I had a life-changing experience which forever altered my perspective.

For the previous two and a half years, I had been working full-time, going to school at night and trying to make it as a professional beach volleyball player. Every minute of my life was scheduled; if I wasn't working, I was studying or training.

Eventually, I hit a breaking point. I was graduating from my night school programme and had lined up a new job which would start a few months later. So I quit where I was working and went to Costa Rica for a month. This was back in the days when Costa Rica was wild, remote and still pretty unheard of. One day, during my travels, I was sitting on a remote beach watching the most incredible sunset. It was brilliant pink and gold colours against the most amazing deep blue sky. A buddy of mine and I had been surfing all day and as he was taking a last few waves, I was sitting on a log and watching the waves crash against the beach.

What struck me in that moment was that the waves had probably been crashing against that beach for millions of years – and they would be crashing there for millions of years after I was gone. It made all the things I had been so focused on and worried about in my life seem very small and unimportant in the big picture. That prompted me to ask a very simple but profound question: "Why am I here?" Stated another way: "What is the purpose of my life?"

That started my journey to not only discover what I call my PFE (Purpose for Existence), but also to live in alignment with it every day.

I wish I could say it was an easy transition from there. The truth is that it was a starting point. When I left Costa Rica, despite telling myself to "never forget this", I slowly allowed myself to create another high stress existence over the next five years, perpetually living an over-busy life. Then I disengaged again. I sold almost everything I owned and went to go and see the world again.

It was during that experience of travelling the world for $40 per day, for a year, that I had my "Aha Moment" about the Big Five for Life. The origins of the experience are based in Africa and on something called the African Big Five. The essence of it is about allowing ourselves to select the five things we most want to do, see or experience in this lifetime before we die; the five things that if we do successfully do, see or experience, will make us genuinely feel that our life is all we wanted it to be. Everything above and beyond that is a bonus.

With that clarity in hand, we allow ourselves to allocate all our resources – time, finance, energy – towards doing, seeing or experiencing those five things. Everything else becomes secondary.

These epiphanies changed my life forever. With my PFE, I know which river I want to raft down during my life. Knowing my Big Five for Life allows me to plan the most important ports of call I want to stop at while I'm travelling along the river.

Ever since I gained this clarity and allowed myself to live in alignment with it, my life has never been the same.

Can you briefly explain why is it so fundamentally important for us to know and incorporate our real passions into our daily private and professional life?

Statistically speaking, the average person gets 28,900 days on this planet. Hopefully it is more – sometimes it is less. Those days tick by very quickly. So one of the reasons it's so important for us to know and incorporate our real passions into our life is because if we aren't careful, our days pass by and we find ourselves at the end of our existence, having lived a fraction of the life we wanted to live.

That's a depressing thought. To be very near the end and feel regret over what we could have done – or wanted to do – and didn't.

The most fulfilled people on the planet have some very important things. They have clarity about their life's purpose. They have clarity about their Big Five for Life. And they have a constant connection to those things; it's where they invest their time, energy, emotions and financial resources.

Because of that, they enjoy their life and they feel their life has meaning, which is a wonderful way to live.

What are the benefits to a company that promotes best leadership concepts with focus on their employees' lives, interests and wellbeing?

There are three primary benefits. The first is that when a leader is fulfilling their own life's purpose through the work they do, then their employees do a better job and thus the leader's life's purpose gets fulfilled. For example, if you work in a publishing house which specialises in children's books, and part of your life's purpose is to bring the joy of reading to kids, then you inspire your people to do a better job and the more your life's purpose is fulfilled.

The second benefit is that as a leader, you are either bribing people to come to work to do something they don't want to do, or you are paying them to fulfil their Big Five for

Life. You feel a lot better about yourself when it's the second.

The third reason is that assuming the business model of the company is solid, then companies which focus on their employees' lives, interests and wellbeing end up more financially successful. It's not surprising, really. Profitability is a reflection of productivity and costs. When people want to be at their job, they are excited about what they are working on and they feel respected for their contributions, so they are more productive. Also, in companies with great cultures, the retention rates are very high. People stay for ten, fifteen, twenty years.

Depending on the industry, a typical company will have 15-20 per cent turnover every year. Imagine the cost of having to find, hire, and train a fifth of your employees every single year. Plus, in that environment, productivity is poor. The new people don't know enough to really contribute, and the most experienced people are busy spending their time training the new people.

Taking the time to align people's life and work interests with the work that needs to be done is pretty rare in most companies. It's common in the most successful ones.

What are three mistakes people – and companies – make about how to do successfully what they love, and love what they do?

#1. Most people don't give themselves time – or put themselves in the right environment – to get clear about what they love, and love to do. It's really hard to live in alignment with your life's purpose and fulfil your Big Five for Life when you don't know what they are.

Leaders of companies fall into that same trap. They are so busy with the day to day, they don't get clear either.

#2. Time and time again, people fall victim to "Mad How" disease. They get so caught up in worrying about "how" to do things that they eventually give up. Every "how" is a learning curve or an obstacle and after they encounter the third one, they have used up so much time, energy and other resources that they quit.

A far more effective strategy is to ask the question: "Who?"

Someone, somewhere, at some point in the history of the planet, has done, seen or experienced what you want to do, see and experience. Find out who they are and what they did to make it happen, and then imitate that. You don't have to imitate it forever, but certainly if you do that at the start, it will propel you over the tops of the obstacles which otherwise would cause you to give up.

This concept applies equally well to individuals and leaders within organisations.

#3. Who you hang around with is who you become. Interested in taking your life or your organisation in a different direction? Excellent. It will require thinking and acting differently. Remember, if nothing changes, nothing changes.

The best way to think and act differently is to hang around people who think and act in spirit with what you aspire to. They are already on the path. Start walking with them. This can be done both in person and virtually. Whether you are actually spending time with people, or reading books/ watching shows about them, it's all positive.

What are some actionable takeaways you would like to leave women about change and choosing what is right for them?

I've mentioned a number of them already. Giving yourself time and space to get clear, aligning all your resources with your Big Five for Life, putting yourself in the right environments and with the right people to live the life you want.... so I'd start with those. Then in conjunction with them, I'd add the following:

Start with a sample.

Here's what I mean by that. The brain's primary goal is to keep you alive. This is good and bad. It's good because it can protect you from things which would end your time on the planet. It's bad because it makes the brain reluctant to change. It's like the brain is thinking: "Hey, whatever we did yesterday, let's just do that again because it must have worked. We're still alive!"

The problem with that is change is required if we're going to move our lives from where we are now to where we want to go. If nothing changes, nothing changes.

The trick to getting our brain comfortable with new changes is to start with small little samples and work up from there. I recommend to people that for the first three weeks, they dedicate just five minutes per day to their Big Five for Life. That's it. Just five minutes per day. Watch YouTube videos about one of them. Read a few pages from a book related to them. Do a little searching on the web.

After the three weeks, bump the five minutes up to ten. Then three weeks later bump it to twenty. Then three weeks after that, to forty. This tiering up method allows your brain to get comfortable as you transition from having a list of your Big Five for Life, to actually living your Big Five for Life.

Soon, your brain is enamoured with the minutes you spend in alignment with your Big Five for Life – so much so, it's not only supporting you in that regard, it's actually seeking opportunities for you to spend even more of your minutes that way.

You can find John at www.JohnPStrelecky.com and across social media.

4 WHAT ENTREPRENEUR/ENTREPRENEURIAL SPIRIT REALLY MEANS – CREATIVITY, ENERGY, FREEDOM, FULFILMENT AND SUCCESS!

"...A great entrepreneur is learning every day. An entrepreneur is somebody that doesn't take no for an answer — they're going to figure something out. They also take responsibility. They don't blame anybody else. And they're dreamers in one sense but they're also realistic and they take affordable steps when they can."

- Daymond John

What is the definition of entrepreneurialism?

- Starting new businesses, or getting involved with new ventures or ideas.

- The spirit or state of acting in an entrepreneurial manner.

(as defined by yourdictionary.com)

For me, being an entrepreneur is part of my genes. It is a pleasure, a passion and allows full rein to unbridled creativity. I can't think of anything better...

I am including this chapter here rather than later in the book as I think it is essential to develop our entrepreneurial spirit in all parts of our life. Whether you decide to take the step to creating your own business, or whether you decide to use that same spirit to improve your fulfilment and results as a valuable and dynamic member of an organisation's workforce, is ultimately your choice, but integrating it into your DNA is going to up the potentiality and vibrancy level of all you do.

In your voyage to date, revealing your predeterminations, your beliefs, your self-discovery and finding what you really want, maybe you have roused a passion or sparked an idea for a business. If so, go for it...

My two main companies (in the entertainment industry and then later in real estate/investment) grew from tiny seeds, both times starting by 'helping someone out' with their career or their business because I had the ideas and some of the knowledge of how to do it. More than anything, the ideas excited me; they energised me. I had more ideas flowing, sparking, jumping, crowding into my head.

I also had two other secondary businesses at the same time as the main ones - one was equestrian buildings and the other a fitness and nutrition business. They were easy to organise, great fun and were businesses that really interested me – related to my main passions, hobbies and interests.

Being an entrepreneur and setting up your own business offers you many benefits

- Freedom to do what you want

- You can be where you want, when you want

- You can decide your income by expanding (or not) to the level you wish

- You choose who you work with – if you don't like them, you can say no!

- Mentally, it's stimulating

- Often you don't need much money to get started...

Obviously there are negatives too, so you need to look objectively and do a proper analysis of what is involved. An additional word of encouragement: there are many organisations and associations out there to help and support you with all aspects of starting a business.

Focusing on your entrepreneurial skills, if you prefer the employee route, is another great option. Using your ideas, creativity and energy to create a better position for yourself, include more of your passions into your daily professional life and at the same time, do something positive, productive and innovative for your company. It is a very fulfilling feeling. Also, it gains you the respect and appreciation which allows you to advance in your career. When you apply your entrepreneurialism to your job, in a team or as a leader, you can not only make your own position better and more rewarding, but you can also bring benefits and inspiration to your colleagues, your work projects and the environment in which you all work. Good for you, good for them, good for the company – and often good for the clients!

"Entrepreneurial business favours the open mind. It favours people whose optimism drives them to prepare for many possible futures, pretty much purely for the joy of doing so."

- Richard Branson

It is a pleasure to introduce you to Jo-Ann – very much an entrepreneur and a wonderful role model for all you can achieve, as well as showing us the freedom and fulfilment you gain from allowing your entrepreneurial instincts to develop. When you meet Jo-Ann you can't help but notice her great energy and creativity, her curiosity in everything and her interest in – and support for – everyone around her. Not only is she full of excellent laser-focused ideas to help you achieve your objectives, she invigorates all around her with her shining aura of happiness and positivity.

 ## ASK the EXPERT:

Jo-Ann Hamilton - Expert in female entrepreneurship, United Nations Women 'Empower Women' Global Champion, business feminist, writer and speaker. Founder of SecretBirds, a global membership-based entrepreneurial community for women and girls.

What is the first thing that comes to mind when you hear about women's freedom to choose what they really want to do?

When I hear about a woman's freedom to choose, I first think entrepreneurship. To me entrepreneurship is the ultimate freedom of choice for women – particularly where economics is concerned. Women define entrepreneurship by shaping it into something that works for them at any stage in their lives. This is what makes entrepreneurship so liberating and provides women with a choice to be free.

What inspired you to become interested in women's prospects and entrepreneurship?

I grew up in an entrepreneurial family, so it was something I was exposed to at a young age. It was natural to me so I never thought of it much. However, as I got older and started working – particularly in corporations and male-dominated industries – I started to think more about entrepreneurship and why it is a viable option for women. Witnessing the many experiences of women in the working world was an 'unlearning' process for me and it really heightened my interest in the entrepreneurial space. It made me realise why so many of my relatives – especially the women – pursued it as a career option.

Do you consider women are well adapted to being entrepreneurs and why?

Yes, absolutely. Women are natural entrepreneurs. Entrepreneurs are innovators, creators, problem solvers and adapters. Women are all of these things because of the roles and responsibilities we play in our communities, societies and wider world. Traits such as communication, collaboration and listening are required in order to succeed in the entrepreneurial space. As mothers, sisters, daughters, wives, friends, etc we possess these traits naturally and wield them skilfully throughout our lives. The statistics also show that women build sustainable businesses which in the long term are very successful and highly profitable.

Do you see a difference in women's approach to entrepreneurship compared to men's?

Yes! Firstly, women and men do not start businesses for the same reason. Women tend to start businesses as a direct result of something which affected their lives on a personal level or something which is specifically important to them. Women also pursue industries in entrepreneurship that they are passionate about or which have special meaning for them. From my experience, women's approach to entrepreneurship is underpinned by a consciousness, and there is a level of compassion involved. All this isn't to say that men do not do the same, but overall I believe men are more driven by the bottom line. Women clearly want and need to make a profit, but they also take other factors into consideration when running their businesses. Men also tend to take a very methodical approach to entrepreneurship, whereas many women run their operations instinctively and by what feels right – not necessarily by sticking to defined rules in a high level business plan.

Do you consider being an entrepreneur is – or can be – an advantage for women over more traditional employee roles?

Yes I do – mainly because of the flexibility. Women wear many hats and the roles we play are vast. Entrepreneurship affords women the flexibility to navigate their world more freely and carry out all their duties wearing their multiple hats. Traditional employees have stringent rules and time restrictions which hinder women, especially once become mothers or have to care for elderly relatives.

Moreover, as an entrepreneur one can really implement one's ideas and be as creative as one wishes, whereas a traditional employer may not allow the individual to do that. As an entrepreneur you also control the pace at which you want to grow, whereas a traditional employer will come with a manager, who ultimately determines the pace at which one will grow.

What are the beliefs women often have regarding becoming an entrepreneur?

Because entrepreneurship is portrayed by the mainstream media through a narrow prism, it appears to be very elitist and gives the impression of exclusivity. This, I believe, makes many women believe that entrepreneurship is unattainable. These images and ideas are constantly thrown at women, which reinforces the notion that entrepreneurship is a space which they cannot occupy. This is an external belief, which women internalise, and that then leads to self-limiting beliefs resulting in low confidence and self-doubt about whether they can or will be successful as entrepreneurs. I also think many women believe that if they work hard and keep their heads down, somehow they will be rewarded by their employer – but we know this is not the case. We have been taught our entire lives that hard work pays. So this is what many of us stick to and you will find that it takes a breaking point for a woman to leave her job behind to start a business. In many instances, women are forced out or made redundant, which leads to them becoming entrepreneurs – not by choice, but as a matter of survival.

What are three mistakes people make due to these?

Firstly, they never pursue their idea because they have bought into the notion that it is impossible to do it. Secondly, they do not seek out the support systems available to them and lastly, they give up too easily – not realising that perseverance and failing are all a part of the entrepreneurial process. Those women who have no choice tend to adapt very quickly because it really comes down to paying the bills, so the mistakes are recognised as a part of the process.

What are some actionable takeaways you would like to leave women about overcoming these, change and choosing what is right for them?

I would like to encourage women to pursue their idea. The only person who has to believe in the concept is you, and once you believe you are bringing something valuable to the market, this will show and others will also buy into the idea. They should seek out networks with like-minded women who are building businesses. This type of peer-to-peer support – whether through mentoring, accountability or collaborative sessions – is so crucial for women, especially in the beginning stages of their businesses. Also, do not give up; there will be many obstacles but it is all worth it in the end. There is no such thing as a bad idea – just an idea that needs some changing to make it work, so pay attention to what the market is saying and respond to it quickly. Ultimately, you have to trust that you are doing the right thing for you and those around you. Once you do, everything else will fall into place.

Why is career fulfilment important – particularly in regard to entrepreneurship?

As human beings our desire is to be fulfilled, to feel complete and whole. As women, we want to feel we are contributing to something which is bigger than ourselves and which is helping others in some way. We are natural givers and caretakers, so this is special for us. I believe that if we are going to spend so much of our time working, it should be doing what makes us feel alive and provides that something special. Entrepreneurship is the perfect avenue to do this as it gives women the opportunity to curate their own lives, based on their own values as opposed to the values of an outside force.

5 CHANGE, FREEDOM, HAPPINESS, FULFILMENT
– YOU ARE WHO YOU CHOOSE TO BE...

"Life is a great story...
It's just that some people don't realise they are the
author and they can write it however they want."

- John P Strelecky

So you are the author – how are you writing your story? Who do you choose to be? After completing the analysis and exercises in chapters one and two, what is the next step?

Now, you have to start thinking selfishly. I don't mean being selfish in relation to other people, but thinking of yourself and what changes to make. You have discovered what is going to make you more fulfilled; you found out the key things that you would like to do.

Now you have to decide if, in fact, you are going to change. If so, how are you going to change? And how important is it? Remember, the practicality of it is different from the image. You have to become very down to earth, lay out what you already have, what you want, where you will find it and what else is needed in order to succeed with this change.

How to decide what should be changed and how it can be done

Start with what frustrates you the most and what you are doing now that is furthest away from what you want. Change that first. You will feel better, more positive, more productive, energised and generally lighter in spirit with the removal of each frustrating item.

You need to work out what is absolutely essential in your daily life – what you truly can't do without – and then start changing some of the other things. That's really how you can prioritise other items as well – on a sliding scale from indispensable down... So for knowing what to do first, think of the essential.

For example – if you need to pay the bills, you need to have a job or some kind of revenue-generating business. You need to ensure that you have to have enough income from your current or a transitional job so that you can keep going while changing. You need to think about whether you have to incorporate anything specific to ease changes regarding your family life and current organisation concerning them. It's really laying out a list of what the possibilities are, and what the impact of each decision or action would be – and then deciding where to go next.

How to decide what is most important and what will have the most effect, and the steps needed to put this into practice

Get a piece of paper and divide it in two columns... Head the columns "pros and cons," "this is good/this is bad," "I hate this/I like this" or whatever speaks to you. Note down what you have now which is going well, and which is linked to what you want to do; then cross out the items you hate or the ones that seem least important, and start focusing on the positives.

By doing this it is easy to see what you actually need to do and what you need to modify. Make an analysis – a really in-depth one. For each item, ask yourself, "If I do this, what effect is it going to have? What potential problems could there be because of it?" That is really the first step to putting your ideas and discoveries into practice because you become aware of what the different choices are.

Prepare yourself for imagining there may be potential resistance or hurt feelings – or not – from your nearest and dearest; frequently we get this back to front. You envisage that some things can seem very hard but often it's self-sabotage. When you are in the habit of doing something, it can be difficult to step out of your comfort zone.

Another example of this – a lot of the time we think it might hurt people if we decide to act in a certain way when in fact, these people are completely oblivious. In reality, all people are actually very self-centred – not necessarily in a nasty way, but they just think of themselves before they think of anyone else.

Frequently we think, "Oh my God I can't do this; it's going to really hurt x," when the person you are thinking of isn't even aware of it. They're doing their own thing in their own little world and they have no idea at all of what you're doing. If they do notice, usually they react, "Oh yes, you want to do that? Nice! Sorry I'm a little busy at the moment..." and go on to their own next priority.

You may have these and other ideas enter your head about possible negative impact on career, life, relationships... To overcome these, it's a very good idea to do "The Fear Exercise" because that helps you sort out your absolute priorities and the main obstacles in your way that are impacting on your decisions. Once you know this, and also the things that you really want to avoid at all costs, you can then decide what limits to put in place.

Exercise 4: The Fear Exercise

1. Identifying ego blocks

This is a really simple exercise. Download the worksheet from the resources section http://unstoppablegoddess.life/ book-resources/ or, get a piece of paper and a pen, or open a document on your computer, and write down any fears or reservations you are having about finding and living your purpose. If you were to find it right now, why might that be a problem? If you lived your purpose from this moment forward, what could possibly go wrong?

2. Worst-case scenarios

Ready? Do you have your list of fears, concerns and reservations? The parts of your psyche that are most concerned about finding your purpose usually employ "worst-case scenario" thinking. That is, they look at each risk in terms of the worst possible thing it could lead to.

This method uses those worst cases to deal directly and effectively with your fears and concerns.

To understand how this process works, let's take a common fear. Many people have the fear, "What if I can't make money doing my purpose?" This is a perfectly valid question. The problem isn't that you have the question – it is that you have never answered it. Well, what if you found your purpose, did it, and didn't make any money on it? What then? If you knew the answer, then you would have a plan. If you had a plan, you wouldn't need to worry. If you didn't need to worry, then getting really clear about your purpose wouldn't be a problem.

This exercise will deal very directly with each fear you identified. You must do it with each and every fear, and you must follow the directions precisely.

1. *You will need the list of fears from the first part of the exercise.*

2. *Start with the first fear from your list. Ask yourself, "What's the worst thing that could happen if this came true?" Write down the answer. Be specific, and make sure it's the worst thing you can imagine. Don't worry about whether it's realistic or not.*

3. *You now have a new, deeper fear. Re-read your answer, and then ask the question again: "What's the worst thing that could happen if that happened?"*

4. *Keep repeating Step 3 until one of the following happens:*

   a. *You start to repeat yourself (ie, the thing you come up with is essentially the same as the answer you* wrote down the last time you asked yourself the question).

b. Your mind is completely blank because you are unable to think of anything worse. (Hint: For most people, dying is NOT the worst thing they can imagine happening to them. Don't stop there! If you died, what's the worst thing that could happen then? Or, what could be worse than dying?)

c. You conclude that it's actually not a problem at all; you would be okay if this happened. (An example of this: A woman in a workshop once said, "My fear is that if I found and lived my purpose, my husband might leave me. What's the worst thing that could happen if he left me? Well, he's a total jerk; I guess it wouldn't really be a problem if he left!")

5. If you repeated yourself or couldn't think of anything worse, continue to work with this fear. Now ask yourself, "If I knew that this would happen if I tried to find and live my purpose, would I still want to?" It doesn't matter what the answer is; all that's important is that you have a clear "yes" or "no" – "maybe" is not helpful. Very important: If you answer "no", you can still find your purpose, so don't worry about it.

6. If you answered "yes", you are complete with this fear. Go back to Step 2 and start working with another one.

7. If you answered "no", ask yourself, "At what point would I stop pursuing my purpose if this fear started to come true?" Write down the answer to a new list called "Constraints". For example, if your fear is that you

wouldn't make enough money doing your purpose and might end up dying of AIDS in an alley, the point at which you stop might be something like, "If I can't pay the mortgage on my house and feed my family, I'll stop doing my purpose and find some way to make money". In this case, you would add the following constraint to your list: "I must be able to pay the mortgage and feed my family." This constraint is a condition of pursuing your purpose. You are now complete with this fear; go back to Step 2 and start working with another one.

8. *Once you have repeated this process with ALL of the fears on your list, ask yourself whether you have missed any fears. There might be one or two more; it's important to be thorough! Repeat the process with any additional fears you can think of.*

9. *Once you've processed all the fears you can think of, read the list of constraints from Step 7.*

10. *Ask yourself, "If none of these things happen, do I choose to find and live my purpose?"*

11. *Once your answer is "yes" or "no" you are complete.*

NB. Download the worksheet that goes with this exercise and other resources here: http://unstoppablegoddess.life/book-resources/

How do you know if you are being honest with yourself?

This is something that comes with practice and with constant analysis of, "Do I really want it?" "Is it an unconscious reaction from a predetermination?" or "Am I thinking/doing this because of appearances/fears/constraints?"

If any of your decisions/conclusions make you still ask, "Why?" "Can I go further?" or "How does it make me feel?" and you don't have a clear answer, then you probably still have some work to do on yourself for real clarity and honesty. When you reach the absolute deepest level and there are no more answers for the how or why, you've got down to the reality.

In what way does this help?

It gives you far more freedom – freedom of choice. If you know that you're being totally honest with yourself, your decisions and actions are made from a strong base – from a position of confidence and power. You know why you're doing something and why you want to do something. With that you can better analyse your objectives, your direction, any potential impact or consequences and how you will manage these in the future. This allows you to decide to what extent you will proceed when choosing if you want to change something or not.

What is non-negotiable?

When you do the fear exercise, if you do it properly, you will find what your deepest limit is – what you really cannot go beyond; what is your worst nightmare. Once you have this knowledge it helps you decide what is not negotiable.

For example, my worst fear is living on the street – no longer having a house. For me, in changing a job or changing any business dynamics, what is non-negotiable is that I must still earn enough money to be able to pay the rent or the mortgage.

Then, what is secondary?

If we carry on with a similar scenario, having enough money to pay the mortgage is essential. As a secondary priority, maybe it isn't essential to go on holiday – but it is essential to have a car. So with these graduations, you can see what you change and what you don't. All depends on your biggest fears, your objectives and then negotiating your choices between what really does have to happen and what doesn't.

For example, I would love to live on a mountain far away from anyone, with no technology, internet, telephone, with beautiful views, completely immersed in nature and not do anything other than go riding and hiking, enjoy the peace and my freedom. However, that's not going to give me any food, so, we have to be realistic sometimes.

Once you've decided what is non-negotiable, what is secondary, where you want to go etc, you can then start to put into place a realistic idea of how to make them happen. This gives you the focus you need for your path. You need to go one step at a time and work out how to get there – who you know, what you need to do, etc. It gives you a game plan.

Where does success come in all this?

Success is fulfilment as we said at the start of the book. Fulfilment/success can be many things – it depends on you. For some people, success is more material and in these cases, they achieve fulfilment from having a specific title at work, having the latest car or having the biggest triumph.

For others, it's finding peace, serenity or calmness. It might be being incredibly fit and healthy. So success is what you define it is as being – for you. The important part of knowing **your** success is that it is your truth, your choice, your feeling and your passion – not someone else's. Sometimes we can spend our whole lives living through another person's ideas of success and not realising it. This is why I am so insistent on doing the previous exercises to really get to the depth of knowledge of yourself, your beliefs, your reasons for doing things and your own passions. Once you have done that, and once you have that knowledge, the success you achieve is your very own – it is what makes you feel that you have reached the best of yourself.

How do you know if this success is personal?

Generally, you know by the feeling you have when you think of 'it', whatever 'it' is. If you feel warm, if you feel energetic, if you feel peaceful, if you have contentment at the thought of it – then it is your success. If you aren't worried about what other people are thinking about, it is really you!

If you are concerned about what someone else will think about your choice then you haven't quite got there yet; you haven't fully discovered your own vision. It isn't your choice of success if you are still worried about outside influences. If you are thinking, "Yes this is me, I feel totally comfortable with it," it's a pretty good chance that it is your success.

Change and evolution can give rise to conflict from unexpected places.

Sometimes you find that people – not always your nearest and dearest but your friends or acquaintances as well as colleagues – are scared of you changing. You may be met with conflict because they are worried or insecure, feeling threatened by your success. It may be they think you will forget them or no longer find them interesting; it may be that they no longer feel good enough. In this type of situation, you simply need to be discreet. There is no need to tell everyone all about your life – particularly if it could seem hurtful or as though you are showing off. Be gentle with your explanations and accept that we don't all want the same from life; we don't all have the same values and ambitions so not everyone understands what we are doing or why. It isn't important – what goes on in someone else's head is their business – not yours. Only what goes on in **your** head is **your** business.

Basically, finding true fulfilment and success comes from you. Other people cannot give it to you – their thoughts or acceptance don't govern you. How much you let them into your life is your choice.

If someone is being aggressive about your choices, or really doesn't want you to move in your chosen direction, then you have to decide: at what stage does their reaction make you unhappy?

The best way is to remain calm and try to explain things, promoting the idea of open-mindedness, etc. You don't have to be antagonistic or defensive, because people have their own thoughts and views. If you want to talk and you think there is going to be a problem, try explaining it from a third person (neutral) point of view.

If it becomes tense, be sure that instead of saying, "You are..." or "You're wrong...", make it more personal to you. "I feel this," "I feel that," "It seems to me," which is a non-conflictual approach – in fact this is a good tactic to use in any situation where there is a difference of opinion with someone.

But again, I can't stress enough that you don't have to tell everyone everything that happens in your life. We aren't competing on Facebook to see who can change their status the most often by posting every detail of their existence. There are some things that we can just peacefully keep to ourselves.

Does this mean leaving people behind in order to achieve our aims?

Sometimes, yes, but it might simply mean changing the interaction we have with them.

If there is a potential impact on someone very close to you, with whom you've got a good relationship, normally you can talk about your wishes and explain why you want this or what you think it will do for you; in what way it will be positive.

You can talk objectively about the advantages and the opportunities. Normally, when you do this with someone who truly wants the best for you, they will be okay.

You might physically leave them behind because they may be in a different geographical location or a different department at work, or they might have a different focus on their career which will mean you are moving in differing directions. But emotionally and psychologically, you can continue to have that same good relationship with them.

So in reality, whether you leave people behind or not depends both on you and the other person. Not everyone is going to support you; not everyone is going to be happy about it. People have their own insecurities, frustrations and problems which can be projected onto you, because they see that you're going forward and they don't have the courage or opportunity to do the same.

Integrating Essentialism as a focus for change and how it helps

'Essentialism' is a book that I highly recommend (by Greg McKeown). The ethos of this book explains the benefits of really cutting down to the essentials to give you more freedom and less stress. This is because a lot of the time, we over-organise. We do too much and we over plan. We think too many things. All this over-activity ends up blocking us from doing anything.

So along with the ideas you have discovered in finding what you really want to do, choosing how to do it and what you might have to change, take into account essentialism in all aspects of your life. Think about what is happening now or what will happen in the future, and how you want to get to your new objective.

Try to become an essentialist – remove everything that isn't absolutely necessary because by doing that, you gain so much more freedom. Think about it in conjunction with this little exercise about visualising.

Visualising for reinforcing the vision of fulfilment and success. What does your future look like?

To keep focus and clarity – as well as to boost your motivation on those days we all sometimes experience when we don't feel quite up to par – you need to project a vivid and detailed image in your brain of where you are going to be and what you will be doing.

To do this, see yourself in the picture in action doing it. Hear what you and others in the picture are saying; fully experience your feelings… Psychologically, this prepares your brain and creates familiarity and belief, making it much easier to actually take your chosen steps. It also gives you a reality check between your ideas and where you are now, helping you to determine the steps in between.

So a mental image is very productive. It helps you analyse what the differences are. It helps you take one step at a time in the right direction.

Emotional benefits of making your choice to change

Emotionally, the knowledge of having taken your decision to change will help you feel free and proceed more happily along your transitional route. You know the direction you are moving in, and you know you can do it. You can see the image of yourself in action – confident and competent, enjoying your life. You will find that knowing you are integrating your passions and new projects will mean you feel – and have – less conflict and less self-doubt in your current daily life. Your confidence will grow. You will feel calmer. When you have a stressful situation at work, instead of taking something badly – feeling that it's a personal attack or you're not capable of doing the task set you – you'll be able to regain equilibrium more quickly and easily. It will give you an added strength.

The physical benefits of making your choice to change

Physically, there can be many different types of effect on you. You might have geographic movement, going to a different area or a different region. Not only that, the effect can often be that you have more physical energy and feel less tired. All of this makes a difference in the way you move; in the way you hold yourself. It increases your activity levels. Overall, your body feels better.

Remember what I said right at the beginning: for the deepest fulfilment, we need to welcome the value of the whole mind-body experience. When every aspect is in harmony and flow, the greatest success and happiness are obtained. Therefore, healthy mind, healthy body! Incorporating all areas – mental, physical and emotional – will give you the optimal results for fulfilment and success.

This means if we include health, fitness and mindset as being integral parts of the whole, we have a far greater capacity for achieving our objectives of freedom and fulfilment – the healthy mind/healthy body I talked about earlier. You will probably see increased levels of health and fitness in all aspects.

May I introduce you to Stina, a wonderful role model for us all for innovation, inspiration and motivation. Her career is a great example of knowing what you want and creating the opportunities for succeeding both as an entrepreneur and business developer.

EXCEPTIONAL WOMEN: Success Talks...

An interview with: Stina Ehrensvard

CEO, mother and innovator in internet security. One of the top 50 most inspiring women in European technology, Female Executive of the Year, Swedish Innovation Award, Woman of Influence, Leading Woman Executive and many more awards...

Where and how did your career begin?

I have always loved cooking and creating things with my hands. At the age of 19 I had my first job as a chef at a small restaurant. A few years later I got restless and started studying industrial product design at college. In the last year of my education, Jakob Ehrensvard, a brilliant electronic engineer, built a working prototype of one of my designs, and I knew this would be my future partner in work and life. Other men had offered nice dinners and flowers, but a working prototype made me really happy! Since then we have been working closely together in the crossroads of IT, design and innovation.

Was it an easy progression?

In one of our innovation projects we learned that more than a trillion dollars are lost due to online identity theft. At the time we did not have a solution, but I knew this was an important mission, and started Yubico to address the problem. The first years were tough, but after eight years I had progressed from being the CEO of a one-man company to something bigger and cooler.

Why the fascination with IT/tech?

The internet is the collected consciousness of all human beings. It is the most powerful communication tool ever created by mankind, and it needs to be protected to stay open and safe for everyone.

How did you find career opportunities for women in your sector/industry?

There are few women who are genuinely interested in internet security. But the ones who are will get a job, as there is a strong market demand.

Tell us more about your company and how you started it...

Yubico's core product is the YubiKey, and our vision is a ubiquitous security key to all internet. When we started eight years ago, most organisations and internet users were not concerned with hacked passwords. Today, this has changed. We started in Stockholm, Sweden, and four years ago Jakob and I moved to Silicon Valley to work closely with the internet thought leaders on a new, open authentication standard named U2F – Universal 2nd Factor. Just like the mobile phone standard GSM connected phones and users all over the world, we want to secure users and services all over the world from identity theft. And the vision is becoming a reality.

You seem to have endless energy and a quest for innovation – what inspires you?

As a little girl I loved building tree houses with my friends and I have always loved creating new things with great people. In the early days at art college I considered the path of a free artist, but then realised that I was more intrigued with solving real problems, and designing products that were useful to people. To be part of a team helping secure the internet is the most inspiring job I ever had.

The Inspiring 50 is a wonderful initiative. Congratulations on being one of the top 50 women in technology! Do you believe this initiative and others like it will help improve acceptance of women at the top and relegate gender discrimination to the past?

I recently read an article that showed that major tech corporations led by women have achieved great results – in some cases better than similar companies led by men. We are all grateful for getting recognition for the work we do, but it is the hard business facts that will have most impact on future gender equality.

So what would be your advice to women hoping to advance in their career?

Ask yourself what makes you really happy and what you really love doing. If you then pursue that route with kindness, passion and determination, your career is likely to unfold naturally.

What, for you, are the obstacles and prejudices that you might encounter as a working woman?

I grew up in Sweden with loving parents and never felt I had less power than my two brothers – or any other boy of my own age. When running my company there have been situations where senior men were confused and uncomfortable with a younger woman in charge, but I have learned I cannot please everyone.

What type of experience do you think is necessary to succeed in your industry? Are there any specifics that are particularly helpful for getting ahead?

Almost a century ago, Dale Carnegie wrote a book where he summarised the number one common dominator for successful people: *The ability to deal with people.* The book is named "How to Win Friends and Influence People" and is full of great advice for getting ahead in any industry.

What differences exist for the younger generation and their opportunities for the future?

My grandmother's job was to have a clean home and serve her husband and children. I am grateful I was offered more options, and I am optimistic about my daughter's future.

Your country, Sweden, and Scandinavia in general are known for their support – and active implementation – of gender balance/parity. Have you noticed a big difference in attitude between different countries and cultures on this topic?

Yes. Although I now enjoy a life in California, I was blessed to grow up in Sweden, where Jakob and I have also raised our own three kids. I often have to remind myself that the gender equality I take for granted is not yet the reality for many women here in USA or other parts of the world.

A year ago I was invited to deliver a fifteen-minute keynote speech summarising my entrepreneur journey. Please feel free to watch it here: https://www.yubico.com/2014/05/the-yubico-entrepreneur-journey/

My best advice is summarised at the end of the video:

"Don't let anyone define what you can or cannot do. Trust your gut and do it!"

6 DEFINE YOUR PURPOSE, PLAN YOUR ROUTE, CREATE YOUR BRAND

What do you do now?

Now we have reached the real outlining and planning stage. Think of this as you would a project – a new project at work where you are putting the management structure in place. Now is the time to work out the different stages: what you already have, what you need to acquire and what can be adapted.

Start by doing a personal SWOT analysis.

Exercise 5: PERSONAL SWOT

(Strengths, weaknesses, opportunities, threats)

A personal SWOT analysis is essential for everyone who wants to progress in their life and career. Just like the SWOT analysis you use in business for your company – for planning expansion, developing new products, marketing strategies etc – this is an excellent tool for yourself. I would say it is indispensable when you are planning any changes in your direction.

For anyone not familiar with SWOT, it is a strategic planning tool that was created back in the 60s. It is still one of the main tools used today to identify and improve the internal strengths and weaknesses of – and external opportunities and threats to – a business or person. It is an excellent idea to make this a habit and do it once every year, because we are constantly evolving...

It is of enormous benefit to you because it lets you evaluate your personal appeal and skillset in a unique way, which then gives you a clear and exceptional opportunity to take concrete action in a valuable and productive manner.

You need to complete this SWOT analysis with the ultimate focus on yourself – for yourself. Then list what should be acted on now, soon or later on. Then ACT on that list and manage your progress.

There are several keys to doing this well, which you must take into account in order to get the best results and not waste your own time.

The main keys are:

1. You need a goal or target in mind. (You already have this, because you have defined your idea in the previous chapters). Use this as the focus for all the following.

2. Think of as many questions as possible for all the quadrants – the more the better. As a basis, these are essentials, but it needs to be YOU who answers them!

   - **S** – Strengths: What are my skills, attributes, assets, resources?

   - **W** – Weaknesses: What areas do I need to improve?

- *O* - *Opportunities: What external changes, (eg social, contacts, tech, development) will give me opportunities?*

- *T* – *Threats: What negative aspects are there in my area of interest?*

3. *Get ideas and input from everyone, everywhere on potential questions and their vision, but make sure it is still you who is answering the questions.*

4. *Make sure you don't have the same thing in different boxes – ie a weakness can't also be a strength; a threat can't be an opportunity.*

5. *Look at your threats before your opportunities, as this can open up your brain to ideas you had never considered before.*

6. *ACT on your SWOT. It isn't there just to look pretty and so you can say you have done it; it is to give you laser focus for your action.*

7. *Monitor and target your SWOT progress – once you have completed your personal SWOT, put the results on a mind map and then give yourself a target for each item you want to change or improve. Take action and revisit your mind map every two or three months.*

8. *Favour continuous evolution – update, ie find new things about yourself, and changes/improvements to make on a regular basis, every six months to a year...*

9. *DO NOT PROCRASTINATE! Don't put it off until tomorrow; as a great Spanish proverb says "Tomorrow is the busiest day of the week!"*

OK, so now put the book down and get going – do your own personal SWOT analysis.

NB. You will find a downloadable worksheet as well as a list of possible questions to ask yourself in the Book Resources section of the website http://unstoppablegoddess.life/book-resources/

If I can see an area that's weak, what should be done about it?

You need to analyse any weak areas, to discover how much they could affect what you want to do. Do you have any existing skill close to the weakness that you can use to build up into a strength? Or is it something that you actually need to correct and therefore find/learn the skills to do so?

Sometimes you might be able to compensate or delegate in order to avoid having to do some things. Being aware of the weakness is already constructive, as it gives you the knowledge necessary to look for additional options.

Does this mean having to learn extra skills?

It could do. Sometimes you need to learn or acquire new skills. For example, if I suddenly decided that I wanted to work as a graphic designer, I would need extra skills because I don't have a clue about what it takes to be a good one. However, if I wanted to go into something more specific with marketing, event management or publicity, then I might be able to adapt some of the skills I already have.

So what you need to do is look at just how far away your goal is from what you already have. If it is a completely new vocation that requires specific skills, then yes, maybe you do need to learn extra ones.

So what would I need to learn?

You need to analyse what you have and what is demanded by the job. To help you with that, use the "Hedgehog" concept. This helps you compare your talents/skills.

Exercise 6: The Hedgehog Concept

The Hedgehog Concept uses the power of simplicity for success. In Jim Collins' book 'Good to Great: Why Some Companies Make the Leap...and Others Don't', he introduces us to the Hedgehog Concept, saying it's "not a goal to be the best, a strategy to be the best, an intention to be the best, a plan to be the best. It is an understanding of what you can be the best at. The distinction is absolutely critical."

Isiah Berlin borrowed from an ancient Greek parable when he divided his world into hedgehogs and foxes. "The fox knows many things, but the hedgehog knows one big thing."

The big advantages the hedgehog has are simplicity and focus! It has one simple, clear vision which drives everything it does, so it does things well and succeeds against all comers.

Why is all of this useful to us? Because all the great companies and the most successful people are, to one extent or another, hedgehogs. They understand and practise what they can be best at. By comparison, companies – or people –

who never gain the same advantage tend to be foxes; they are more dispersed, extended and divergent.

You will get the greatest freedom, the most fulfilment and the best success if you do the same – follow the hedgehog concept.

The concept needs you to make three separate assessments. These lead you to create your strategies on a deep understanding of three dimensions and three circles, and then translate that understanding into a straightforward, crystal-clear concept to shape your efforts. This is why it is called the Hedgehog Concept.

You use your deep understanding of the intersection of these three circles to create your greatest flow.

1. *What are you deeply passionate about? In other words, what makes you look forward to getting up in the morning and starting your work? What makes you stay late? What do you really believe in doing?*

2. *What you can be best at in the world – you have a skill or talent you feel you were born to do*

3. *Where is this good at generating revenue? Where will you be well paid for doing this – for your dream?*

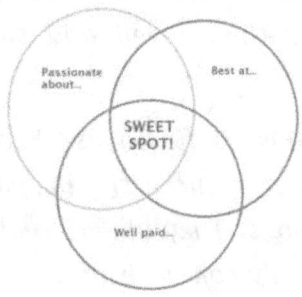

The optimal way forward for you is the 'sweet spot' in the middle, at the intersection of the circles.

Start thinking about this, and use your personal SWOT analysis and the results of the other exercises to help you. It might not be obvious right away, but if you use it in conjunction with the other results, gradually a clear picture will develop showing you where you can have your one central focus. Then align your strategy, your communication and your direction to reflect your true passion, talent and income-generating potential. This will provide you with long-term focus and guide you towards fulfilling long-term success.

NB. Download the worksheet that goes with this exercise and other resources here
http://unstoppablegoddess.life/book-resources/

How to prioritise and organise your goals, and develop your strategy

You need to put down all the results on paper. Normally, if you're doing the SWOT, you will be answering various questions, plotting things on a graph, spreadsheet or preferably a mind map and coming up with lists. Take all of these and see where you already have the skills and opportunities, or something very similar and adaptable. Then, from that, decide what you need to do next.

You already have most of the results from the exercises you've just done. Ascertain which are the easiest to put into action. Get in your head a plan of when you want to incorporate your new actions and where. Find out what is available that can help you in your chosen direction and decide. At the same time, organise and prioritise your goals.

Look for the overlap – at what works together. It becomes clear when, for example, you look at what you're deeply passionate about, combined with your strengths from the personal SWOT. You can see what goes with – and complements –what. Say to yourself: "Therefore, as part of my strategy, I need to balance this and focus on something else." Obviously, it's very personal.

But think of it as a project management exercise at work. Apply it to yourself and your career. Then think of your network, the contacts you have and the people you know who might be able to help you. If you need to acquire new skills, search to discover where you can learn them. Give yourself a time span.

Planning the stages of your plan and the timing

You need to work out what will be the easiest and the most difficult to achieve. Then put these points in what seems to be a natural order for your own situation – you don't want to avoid doing something, but you don't want to kill yourself by doing too much at once either.

Put things that naturally go together - for example new skills training - into the same stage and same timeframe. You could do this with a timeline as you would in a work project – create a simple one in excel and then look at the timeframe for new skills training. Realistically, how much time is free to study and then how long will it take to get the desired qualification? If it might take too long for career progression, then consider alternative options: fast track training or reducing another hobby short term

Make sure you take into account your overall normal life – what you're doing at work; what you're doing at home. Make life easy for yourself.

Be sensible. If you know you're going away on holiday, there's no point in trying to organise something which requires you to be in front of the computer in your office to do it. Be logical about planning.

Don't leave your brain behind. You need to think. Think of it as an external exercise. If you were going to mentor someone else, what would you advise them to do? By adopting that thought train, very often you'll find the clarity to make it easier for yourself.

How much do you need to change, adapt and ultimately, where do you start?

How long is a piece of string? This depends on where you want to end up in the long term. Start off with small steps; aim for minimum change to begin with. You don't need to make a huge step all at once. Change the minimum so you feel comfortable with that and can integrate it well.

What can you adapt? Basically, anything that seems close or linked to what you're already doing because quite often, we are already doing some things that we quite like. We just need to refocus the way that we do them.

Start with smaller changes you can make in the right direction so that you keep it simple. If you try something that's incredibly complicated, you're setting yourself up for problems. When you set up something simple, you can just take one little step. Do it. Succeed at it. You build your confidence. You feel pleased. You pat yourself on the back. You're actually creating the habit of getting bigger and better.

So don't fight yourself. Don't give yourself problems. Start with simplicity and one step at a time. It's going back to essentialism. Do something that's simple and makes you feel good.

What about getting support at work? How do you know who's on your side? Is it reasonable to talk to somebody in HR, your boss or a colleague?

This is always a delicate issue. The majority of what you're doing will either be applied to – or have a strong impact on – work and your career, so you need to think carefully about this.

If it's something that is going towards improving your career and getting a higher position, I would say yes, you can get support at work. If it's aimed at stealing your immediate boss' job, it's probably not a good idea to ask him to help you!

But if it's something that can have a good impact on your team – for example an idea for promoting the systems that work, etc – yes, talk to your boss or talk to a colleague. If you have a colleague who seems open-minded and positive, maybe have a discreet conversation with them first to see what they think. Also, see what they think the opinion of the rest of the company might be.

Sometimes, if you have a very radical or innovative idea and you work for a boss who likes being progressive, you might be able to have a brainstorming meeting or set up something more radical, so you can get great things done in this way. It depends on the company and the company culture.

Human Resources. I find you can have different types of HR. Sometimes they're absolutely great; they're very supportive and amazing. At the moment, I work with two HR directors I think are heaven for any person who wants to progress, because they're really open-minded. They're very supportive.

But also, you can have the other side of the coin where there are jealous, small-minded elements who really give the impression that they are the HR mafia. So be sensible; don't think that everyone is going to be your ally.

If there is someone around you who has done something unusual or different, they might be a good person to talk to because they're already more open-minded; plus they may well have come up against problems and succeeded in overcoming any difficulties.

So, to recap, have a look at who is around you. If you have a good feeling with them, if you feel inclined to confide in them, if you feel a sensation of trust with them then probably yes, talk to them. Some companies offer mentoring schemes, either within the company or outside. That could also be a good avenue to pursue.

So how long will it take and what happens when there are distractions and diversions? How flexible can you be with the process?

The main point here is that you really need to think about enjoying the journey – and not just obsessing about the destination because of the timescale. Yes, you have to have a vague timescale, but you need to enjoy what you're doing. The whole idea of this book – and the process – is to remove stress, remove boredom and get closer to what makes you feel good. So enjoy what you're doing. Enjoy exploring the avenues.

You might find you can achieve what you want in six months, a year, two years. I would say again, looking back to John and The Big Five for Life, put what you want in your head and then see different ways of getting there, because it's not always directly upwards or forwards.

Sometimes, you will get more pleasure in going sideways or taking a curve instead of a step because it's more interesting. There are more opportunities. There's more variety. So be flexible.

If it seems fun, if it seems interesting, do it! Don't worry about having to move in a slightly different direction. Often we find that natural moves are more rewarding, more interesting and far more successful in the long run than being blinkered and trying to go directly.

Let me introduce you to Ruth, a warm, dynamic, successful woman. Ruth is a strong advocate and supporter of women in business and helping them maximise their career potential, particularly in achieving board level positions. Her experience of working and delivering solutions in the business, government, statutory and non-statutory sectors has helped staff at all levels from junior staff to senior management.

 ## EXCEPTIONAL WOMEN: Success Talks

An interview with: Dr Ruth Sacks

Business Development Director at Westminster Business School and principal lecturer. Creator of programmes: Women for the Board and Cohort 4.

What is the first thing that comes to mind when you hear about women's freedom to choose what they really want to do?

I am delighted that women are assertive and actively choosing their career direction. Women in the 21st century should be able to access constructive and supportive career advice throughout their careers, from whenever they start to think of what they want to do – whether they are seven, seventeen or twenty-seven years old. Career advice is not a one-off. We all change our minds, develop new skills and learn to do things differently, better or with a wider range of skills. So that we can make the most of our learning and continue to progress, there should be more career advice stations at all points in our professional, leading and managerial working lives.

List three pieces of advice you have on obtaining career fulfilment.

- Make sure you regularly ask for feedback about how your ways of working are perceived, and how people like working with you. Think about the feedback you are given and how you wish to act on it – even if you don't like it.

- Recognise what your personal ethical boundaries are – what you will accept and what is not acceptable to you – and always be clear about that.

- However difficult work may be at times, you always need to find something enjoyable every day: something or someone that makes you laugh.

What are three mistakes people make about career objectives?

- thinking that career paths have to be straight lines
- thinking that you have to follow/stick to/stay with the same topic/subject/field all through your career
- thinking that a move to the next stage in your career is only upwards/in one direction.

What are some actionable takeaways you would like to leave women about change and choosing what is right for them?

- Make up your mind – if it seems right to you, grasp the opportunity with both hands and make it yours.

- Don't be afraid to apologise – even if it's not totally your fault. If this incident is likely to follow you through your career in a less than positive manner, then halt it by negotiating a better ending.

- Be positive – even when it seems as if everyone has it in for you, find one positive thing. Repeat it several times and from there, other positive things should come. You might not have changed the situation, but you will feel stronger and more able to cope.

Why is career fulfilment important?

If having a career is important to you, then find what you enjoy doing, keep learning more about it, improving and wanting to get up in the morning to do more. Remember that if your career is an important part of your life, that helps to maintain your fulfilment – but it's not the be all and end all; make time for other things that will create balance and give you perspective

Where and how did your career begin?

I started working full-time in Italy, but whether that was the beginning of my career or whether it started before then with the various Saturday and holiday jobs I had as a teenager – including cinema usherette, shop assistant and pub work – I don't know! I think all my life experience has contributed to the decisions about my working life.

Was it an easy progression?

I was brought up to do the best you can... for me this has meant working hard – that's not always 'easy.'

How did you find career opportunities for women in your sector? Did you have a long-term plan or was it opportunity that forged your career?

My career has developed through periods of steady, regular incremental progression and then twisted or turned through 'accident' or opportunity. I've learnt that it's important to be open to all suggestions; maybe not to say 'yes' straight away but to consider and maybe negotiate adjustments which make the opportunity more interesting

You are currently developing several post-graduate and executive development programmes, including Women for the Board, Leadership Perspectives, MSc Leadership as well as supervising doctoral students. Please tell us more about this...

I am extremely proud of Women for the Board, a six-day session for senior women who want to take the next step. This initiative, which only started in January 2014 but is now running its fourth programme, is a combination of skills development, increasing confidence and learning about the roles and responsibilities of board membership. Amongst a number of topics, we include the legal responsibilities of a trustee and director – executive and non-executive; resilience; using social media; some work on finance and we have head-hunters coming to talk about getting a role. Chief executives, chairs and board members come and talk about their experiences. It's a full programme, giving good preparation to get onto a board. My goal is that within six months of completing the programme, 50 per cent of the participants achieve a significant promotion at work or a board role. We are just collecting the data for Cohort 2. I am delighted to say that 40 per cent of Cohort 1 succeeded within six months.

http://www.westminster.ac.uk/women-for-the-board

Leadership Perspectives is a new series of workshops for all middle to senior managers who would like to refresh or boost to their skills. These are three-hour sessions run by experts in their fields. They aim to be challenging – but at the same time useful –and include practical sessions on a range of topics. Workshops include risk management, creating and selling your vision and nurturing innovation to be usual rather than exceptional. You can see these are stretching topics.

The MSc Leadership is a practice-based part-time Masters. Participants use the projects they are working on professionally to guide their learning about leadership. There are sessions on different aspects of leadership – the challenges and strategies to enhance leadership roles – which participants should be able to relate directly to their own context. We also work in action learning sets as a further opportunity for problem solving and development. Each participant can shape their learning journey. It's a challenging and at the same time a valuable experience, which has been running since October 2015

What did you find the most interesting and challenging part of this responsibility?

I am learning all the time – organisations are changing and the challenges they face cannot be addressed with old-fashioned tools. Now, more than ever, companies are multi-generational, multicultural workplaces. People work face to face as well as virtually across time zones. We need to respect and value difference and respond in ways which support and develop individuals within their working environment – rather than take a 'one size fits all' approach. Obviously we have to be mindful of economies of scale, but current and developing technologies can support this. As a result, executive development has to consider different approaches to learning. A key driver in my role is finding ways to provide such a learning environment and one that meets the needs of 21st and 22nd century organisations

For you, what are the global leadership challenges regarding parity?

This has to be addressed at many levels. Achieving real – rather than token (through quotas) – diversity throughout business communities is not just about who sits in the boardroom, it's about valuing everyone, whatever their working contribution. This may be through a job share, part-time or term-time working – whatever your role in the company. Other facets of this challenge would be identifying role models for all, unpicking and tackling unconscious bias, having affordable childcare.... sadly, it's a very long list. Yet we are making progress and the more we promote our progress, the more others sit up, take note and emulate.

What differences exist for the younger generation and their opportunities for the future?

Work will be a different place, with tools and opportunities that I cannot dream of at the moment. We know that generations X, Y and now Z have different career expectations and aspirations, and they will meet challenges and have opportunities that will partly be based on what is happening now, but may also be completely different. I believe that education is the origin of change – not necessarily through formal means by attending school, but knowing how to be aware of what is happening, having the confidence to ask questions and then find new and different answers. These will be the starting points to open new and different avenues to explore. I hope they enjoy the adventures!

7 OPPORTUNITY AND SUCCESS: BEING – AND BEING SEEN AS – CAPABLE, COMPETENT AND UPWARDLY MOBILE

When you want to progress in your career, you need to look at how success can be achieved, how you can get that promotion and how you can be seen as a rising star or high flyer.

With this, you need to be very positive about what you want to do and where you want to go. Focus is definitely one of the most important aspects of getting success. You need to have your goals – but then you need to be prepared to give more, and put more energy into things. You can't just show up and do it; you have to make people aware of you.

So in order to be seen as the rising star, high flyer and promotion material, you need to do something extra. You need to do something different because you don't want to be seen as one of the sheep – you want to be the sheepdog.

For example, if you've got a group that you're frequently working with, harness your innovation skills and create something to do with them. Create something that's going to help all of them. If there's a project that has something particularly difficult or unusual, be the person who volunteers for it.

If you are the only female director and you want to get onto a male-dominated board, think of an angle that's not going to be typical male-female direct competition – but something that as a woman, you have additional talent for and can share with them from your different vision.

In this, you are not highlighting that a woman can do this or a man can do that. What you're doing is bringing an additional depth to the project or to the table. Use the opportunities available during brainstorming sessions, negotiations and debates. Think of something different.

When it comes to promotion, if you have a traditional company with evaluation reviews once a year, think several months ahead of what the promotions are likely to be, and which one you want. Don't focus completely on the traditional line of advancement. You might well find doing something different – or adding a different skill – will give you the possibility of promotion because you show yourself to be a more rounded individual and therefore a more valuable addition for that post.

Always look to add something extra – and preferably something that's unusual. Think outside the box.

Managing other people for best results

Sometimes as a woman – particularly if you are a young woman – this can be a little complicated. It is ridiculous in this day and age, but you might still encounter older men who don't like working with women as much as with men.

You do come across men who are rather traditional; they might resist because you are a woman but also it could be because they're feeling stressed or worried that you are better than they are, and this makes them insecure.

Another reason can be the difference in mentality and attitude between men and women. Sometimes men just don't understand what we mean or how we think. I know I talk a lot about other books, but think about 'Men are from Mars, Women are from Venus'... we do think differently and we do act differently. It doesn't mean that an individual is right or wrong, or that one sex is more capable or better at doing something. We are just different, and have different ways of looking at things and getting results.

When you are managing a mixed team, you need to take into account that you might say one thing and they might hear another. Particularly when you're at a high level, one of the first things you need to do – because it's absolutely crucial that you're always at the top of your game – is make sure you have personal interaction with all the people in your team. You need to get to know them. You need to be sure they understand you and you understand them. This is one of the fundamentals in gaining a better relationship with them.

If you take the time to really explain and ask questions, encouraging them to ask you questions, potential misunderstandings can be cleared up right from the start.

I know when you are in a high position you tend to have other priorities. You have to make sure the budget is right; you have to manage expansion; you have to set up the new business deal with Hong Kong, etc, but it is imperative to keep this personal touch.

If you become the director behind the door that is always shut, never communicating with anyone, you're not going to know what's going on. You're not going to receive the same loyalty or commitment from people as you will if you keep the door open and make a point of taking the time to get involved with your team and what they are doing.

Interaction and regular meetings are key to good people management. It doesn't need to be a long meeting – it can be a quick ten minutes – but it lets them know that you are there, that you are approachable. Make sure there are no misunderstandings – unintentional or intentional.

Men, older men and decision making

Some say that men are better at decision making. In fact, they tend to make decisions differently. Women tend to hide their light under a bushel and be less directly outspoken about decision taking – particularly in front of groups of people. This can be a problem – not only in gaining promotion but also when leading a meeting.

In decision making, women tend to think all around the question in order to be objective and factor in all the potential risks. Men tend to go straight for the kill and focus on what they want and how they want it. In general, they are much quicker at responding. There is statistical proof that companies with mixed-sex boards outperform those with all-male boards by 26 per cent. Studies have also shown that investments run by female hedge fund managers outperformed those run by men. However, I would say for decision making, the ideal is to have men and women working together.

If you're a woman and you are in the decision making process, use the vision of both men and women. Try and put yourself into a man's brain so you can then see both sides of the argument. Both sexes are talented, skilled and have their own particular strengths, but we work best in collaboration. If you react entirely as a woman, you might miss out on some of the aspects that men might think of. So sometimes, we actually have to be a hybrid of both.

You don't need to leave your gender to one side, but you have to be objective and take advantage of the fact that men and women working well together and in harmony can be very, very strong.

How to be seen as equal to – and 'better' than – male colleagues

You need to present yourself differently. Much of the time we find women and men trying to be clones. Traditionally, a woman trying to go up the corporate ladder will aim to be the clone of one of her male colleagues, because predominantly it's still men who are at the top, so it's normally men making the decisions.

Because we do think differently, it isn't easy to compete on exactly the same levels – and why should we have to? You can show your strengths and skills, and be seen as 'equal' in different ways.

Underline *where* your strengths are and really promote and present *what* they are. Don't try to be completely equal and don't necessarily try to prove that you are better – you want to show your *different* skills. Underline one or two strengths which show different aspects or different vision from your male colleagues. This can make you stand out, and be seen as an expert and talented person. It gives you a more rounded and a more skilled approach – you show different strengths and therefore open up potential for different areas where you can be more productive.

Lack of confidence, insecurity and proving yourself

Women tend to lack confidence more than men do. Please don't shoot me for saying that – we look more objectively at others, then we pick holes in ourselves about where we're not good enough. Men, however, just tend to think, "I'm great at this," and they don't think about anything else. Men, please don't shoot me for saying that either!

When you lack confidence, you need to reassess yourself. You need to see if you really aren't good at something. If that is the case, then do something to improve it. If you're just panicking but you do have the skills, you can do practical exercises to make yourself feel better.

For example, if you feel insecure with public speaking – which a lot of people do – then practise. Literally, if you have a big meeting coming up where you will be talking in front of 200 people, or you're presenting the new budget to the board and the shareholders will be there, then seriously, put yourself in front of the mirror. Turn on the tape recorder. Practise what you're going to say. Listen to how you sound, see where there's a problem and decide what you don't like.

Rehearse it as though you were an actor. Speaking of acting, if you lack confidence or feel insecure, put yourself into the position of being an actor. Play a role. Often, pretending to be the character in that role actually gives you the confidence. No need to panic – instead, imagine yourself as Mrs Super Confident. Tell yourself, "I am being Superwoman today," and really play that role. Stand up straight. Put your shoulders back. Imagine that you've just won an Oscar or an Olympic gold medal, and attack the 'public speaking' situation in that frame of mind.

The benefits of male and female colleagues working together to produce better results

Organise men and women so they work together well. Having a good relationship between them and with you pays dividends. As director of a team, project manager or when setting up a new department, be sure to introduce men and women to the way of working where emphasis is put on understanding and valuing each other's strengths and complementing each other's weaknesses. You will obviously get better results because you are using the best of all their talents and promoting a happy, more appreciative working environment to boot.

The key is to get them to understand each other well, so they can understand why one thinks or acts differently. In this way you are putting the emphasis on their complementary skills. They will be happier together, which means you have better work morale, which gives more energy. This in turn promotes more creativity, which in the long term creates better results for them and better results for you – whatever the project is that you're working on.

It's always very important to be hands on. Really get involved with creating some kind of programme or team building exercise which will generate clarity between your male and female colleagues. This way, they don't feel they're on opposing teams. Instead, they feel that they're equally respected, appreciated and capable, and that working together is going to bring them significant benefits – as well as benefits to you as manager.

Essentials to incorporate and issues to take into account

- You need to have a clearer understanding of the people who work for you.

- You need to look at your team and see the way they work. This will enable you to identify where they've got problems and what you can do to get it working better.

- You need to understand the characters who don't want to work well or fit in. You need to find the troublemakers.

- You also need to find the ones who will work too hard and burn themselves out, because that happens as well and can be just as destructive as someone who is being difficult.

With team creation you need people to work together, so see which characters complement each other.

If you've got two natural leaders, you don't want to put them in head-on competition. It's far more effective to get both of them in different aspects of the group so their strengths are supporting the others within the group.

A main issue you need to take into account is if you have someone destructive in your team. In this case, you have to find a solution urgently. Either you have to remove them from the team, or do something to change their attitude. It is essential to stop any aggression or destructive element that this person might have, because someone like that in a team can be toxic.

Other things to take into account – Sometimes you may come across someone who is lazy, or who always takes the compliments and tries to infer responsibility for what they haven't done.

Unfortunately, with teams you have to be aware of the negative elements as well as the positive. Pretending that everyone is nice or wonderful is not a constructive way of managing a team. You need to be supportive and help them, and you need to be positive – but you also need to be aware that there are two sides to everything and not everything is paradise.

Drawing the line between being a boss and a friend – being nice and still getting respect

This can be a problem because it's always sensitive – particularly if you've been working within a team and have recently been promoted over them. An example would be if you're a group of senior managers and you've just been promoted to director. There's a certain amount of readjustment that has to happen because before, you were their friend and now you're their boss.

The easiest way is to be clear and open. Start by talking about it. You could begin by saying something like, "Okay, maybe we've got to readjust a few things. I would very much like to remain on a friendly basis, but I hope you understand that now that I am the boss, I will have to take decisions that will involve being more directive than maybe I was before, and I won't always agree with everything."

You also need to take into account that you might now be seen as the enemy. Try not to take it personally – be objective. It's life; this is what being a boss is about. You have to accept that there are decisions to be made that won't always be popular. But you need to do it. You need to look at the big picture. Is it going to help the team? Is it going to help the company? Is it going to be a productive decision?

Sometimes you may have a situation where one of your team comes to you with a real problem which they need to talk about – and before, they looked on you as their friend. Personally, I think you should still try and help them and offer a supportive hand. Just because you're a boss doesn't mean you have to become a complete dragon.

In your new position you should be respectful at all times and at all levels, because when you show respect, you gain respect. If you're too 'sugary sweet' and overly nice, they will think you're not capable of doing the job, and also they're going to be suspicious. So don't try and go over the top being nice - be yourself, but accept that a boss is not the same as a friend.

If you are personal friends with someone and you've now become a boss, you can talk together and agree that in work hours, you're the boss so your action is to lead, whereas when you walk out of the door you can be friends again. You stop talking about work and you leave the work relationship behind.

You must try and differentiate between professional and personal.

The challenges of motherhood and finding a suitable balance between having a full time career, being a great mother and still retaining the space to be an individual.

This is one of the reasons why I think being aware of your predeterminations and knowing what you really want is absolutely fundamental to being successful on any level - personal or professional. Being a mum takes a lot of time, energy and emotion.

Children growing up need you to be there; you need to be present. They are amazing, superb and the best. I'm not a naturally gushing maternal woman - I am much more a careerist, but without any shadow of a doubt, my children are the best thing that ever happened to me.

However, as for giving up a career - forget it. I truly couldn't be a full-time mother long-term; I just couldn't. I would go completely crazy. So you need to work out what you want in this domain. You need to know for yourself – without outside pressure – and decide how you are going to proceed.

Some people would prefer to focus on motherhood for a few years and then come back to getting really involved in their career again. Some people don't want to take off more time than the minimum. Neither is right; neither is wrong. It is totally the decision of each individual mother. You just need to think it through and work out the options, as the organisation of each scenario is slightly different.

I made the decision to give up work in my early pregnancy and stay with the children for the first couple of years. I had my children soon after each other – there are only fifteen months between them. Then, when my youngest was eighteen months old, I started a business in a new domain that allowed flexibility with working hours so I could have some time with the children late afternoon/early evening and work again afterwards. They started nursery school when they were about a year old, which freed up a good chunk of work time for me during the day. This allowed me to create the business before setting it up, running it then expanding it. I absolutely loved the business and the way my day was organised... it also made me feel much happier and more confident about my roles both as a mother and a businesswoman. It suited me, but that was me. We are all different and have different styles – the magic is to find your own!

So once you have decided what suits you, you then need to think about how this is going to work with husband, other family, etc. If you want to keep going up the career ladder, seriously having high-flying opportunities, you need to have a very open and serious talk with your husband/life partner.

Make sure that he totally and utterly agrees with you that your career is as important as his. Ideally, he will make as many sacrifices or commitments as you do because – and this is not intended to be negative about men – a lot of men still think their career is more important than yours, because of *their* predeterminations.

The next step is to put an infrastructure in place. Being clear about what is involved is essential. Recently, particularly with differences in the laws on equality and gender balance, many people seem to think that mothers can have a superb career without putting in the same long – and frequently erratic – hours as a man who has the same ambitions.

I don't think you'll find many men with a really superb career who have the time for meeting the kids from school every day, or going out and doing the shopping during the week. With this, I'm not saying either of the sexes is better: I am making –and underlining – the point that if you want a really high-flying career, it doesn't matter if you're a man or a woman. There are certain indispensables: for example, you have to be physically and mentally 'there' in the company and your focus has to be unequivocally on your business. You must be available for an emergency, and be aware of – and deal with – possible problems and decisions which need to be made, etc.

This is not to say you can't be a mother – and a very good, loving and attentive one at that. Succeeding in this is absolutely not a problem. It's no different from being a father – apart from the biological aspect. But a high-flying career doesn't do your private life any favours, whether you're a mother *or* a father. So you need to be aware of that. And you need to decide in advance what your options, your objectives and your limits are – plus how much you want to commit.

If you're both high flyers, you will need great organisation and support. Your children are wonderful, amazing, loving, fun, generous and enormously fulfilling – but they do have needs which you must fully and wholeheartedly support. There are many possibilities to help you and your children in this – right from when they are babies through to teenagers – such as nannies, crèches, nursery schools, child-minders, au pairs and even older family members if they live in the same area as you do. You simply have to be well organised and decide your priorities.

Obviously a part of this is deciding how long you wish to take off for pregnancy, how you will ease back into work and where you will aim for professional progress and advancement on your return to the workplace.

Mentoring is a great help with this aspect. Some companies already have mentoring schemes in place for career progress. You could ask to be mentored by a woman who has already experienced combining pregnancy, motherhood and return to work...

Support mentoring both for manager and team

Mentoring is excellent in many situations – particularly if you have just come back from having a child, or if you've just had a new promotion.

For example, if you're a new VP, the ideal is to have a mentor who has already been there, who has held that position and continued to higher levels. When you have any doubts, you can ask for advice. You can use your mentor as a sounding board.

When you first start in a new role, having a mentor helps you avoid making a fool of yourself in front of your team by asking stupid questions. Personally, I think mentoring is very, very helpful. I could have saved myself a few blushes in the past if I had had a mentor for certain promotions during my career.

The same applies to your team. A mentoring system will really help them to have a totally productive working relationship. So if your company already offers this, great. If they don't have this benefit available, suggest it or organise it yourself. There are many groups and associations that provide mentoring opportunities.

In addition, this is one of those radical ideas that can raise your profile with the boss because it is a positive and constructive action. It creates a happier workforce and results in a more loyal and dedicated team. Everyone feels better, they learn more skills, they become more productive, results are better overall – and, to boot, it reduces stress.

Managing office politics

Office politics are always a nightmare, like any politics. To successfully manage them you need to be very aware of what is going on, so open your eyes and ears. Analyse the situation. Analyse who knows whom. Decide what you think is important and what isn't. Then think hard about situations – such as taking on a new client – where a very sensitive and difficult negotiation is needed in order to achieve a happy result. Try and remove your personal feelings altogether. Accept that office politics are a minefield, and you just have to become a very good acrobat in order to avoid the mines.

Is lateral career change as good as vertical, and how can success be measured on this path?

Personally, I believe lateral career change is actually more productive and more positive than the vertical kind because it opens up different options. It gives you a greater range; a greater scope of achievement. To a certain extent, progress depends on what level you are at and how close you are to your goal.

For example, say you are a vice president of the company and your aim is to become the president. If the existing president seems in extremely good health, is very dedicated to his job and not likely to be retiring or moving on anytime soon, a lateral career change is obviously going to be more interesting and offer you more scope. You don't always have to be focused on 'promotion' and going to another company to get the job you want. You could move laterally and incorporate different aspects of the corporate responsibilities and development.

Adding lateral movement and responsibility is positive. It's very rewarding for you because it ignites your interest, sparks your curiosity and gives you passion and fire – but also, it can open your mind to other ideas. Then at a later date, it can give you the option of many more opportunities because you've become a more rounded person. You've not only acquired additional skills, but it has also been a rewarding and fun experience.

You have already met Louise earlier in the book, with her insight on what freedom and fulfilment mean as a successful businesswoman. Now we hear the inspiring story of how she started and her progress along the way...

 ## EXCEPTIONAL WOMEN: Success Talks

An interview with: Louise O'Sullivan

Former CEO of ANAM Technologies, recipient of the '50 Most Inspiring Women in European Tech' award, Advocate for gender parity in the IT Industry and Strategic Advisor at #techmums

Where and how did your career begin?

I have been working since I left school because training in hotel management requires you to do it in a practical way as well as theoretically.

I started in telecoms/tech in 1995 in a company called Aldiscon in Dublin. It was the halcyon days of tech start-up and it was very exciting and fun. I started in marketing and worked through a number of departments in the company, covering bid management, project and account management. I applied the same principles I had learned in hotels to get to understand how everything worked. You ask questions and use your initiative to improve things or make things happen.

Everyone, including the industry, was learning then so it was a good time to get into telecoms and tech for someone like me who had no technical qualification.

Was it an easy progression?

Easy is not an expression I would ever use to describe anything I have ever done – I have always pursued the more challenging road! The buzz and excitement of telecoms and tech were quite intoxicating at that time and I couldn't resist the opportunity to move into it.

You trained originally at the Shannon College of Hotel Management, so quite a change – why the fascination with IT/tech?

I always wanted to be an engineer, but wasn't very enthusiastic about applying myself academically. I am more a worker than a student. I learn on the job.

When I was growing up I was the one in the house who always knew how all the technology worked (bearing in mind the limited availability at that time) but we had early computers (VIC 20 and Commodor 64) and I spent hours and hours on them, figuring out how to make them do what I wanted. So technology was always in my sphere and it never fazed me; it still doesn't.

I see technology as an incredibly valuable tool that can benefit everyone – especially women and children – and can therefore affect entire communities and societies.

Has the balance/imbalance between men and women affected you?

Not in the early days of my career because I don't think I really noticed it, and I am sure in 1995 there were a lot more women – who hadn't yet had babies – who had just come out of college and were being swept up by all the companies looking for an educated engineering workforce in Ireland at the time. There were definitely no women in decision-making roles at that point. Telecoms and tech were bastions of maleness on the business side, but it was kind of the 'Mad Men' days of technology.

It was in coming back after having had my family and understanding the immense challenges that women face trying to get back into their chosen career whilst being a parent, and being valued, that I really started to take note and I realised how little had changed within those twenty years.

Tell us more about your company and how you turned it around

I turned the company around over the last three years as part of an incredible team of committed and exceptional people – both internally in the company and also through the support and guidance I received from my investors and mentors. So whilst I led the charge, the credit for the success is definitely shared amongst us all.

Following the recession, a lot of companies in Ireland in our space were struggling. We had all of the components but needed some leadership and strategic direction.

The reason I stuck with it was because of the amazing people involved. We have exceptional technology and expertise that deserved a platform, and the market was just beginning to evolve itself so we could build on it.

The Inspiring 50 is a wonderful initiative; congratulations on being one of the top 50 women in technology! Do you believe this initiative and others like it will help improve acceptance of women at the top, and relegate gender discrimination to the past?

I was so honoured to have been included in the Top 50 in Europe. What I particularly like about this initiative is that it is pan-European. I have travelled the world speaking to women and we all have the same issues professionally; it is a borderless issue.

The objective is definitely to relegate gender discrimination to be a thing of the past. The speed at which it happens is the question. You are talking about changing perceptions that are age-old and that is not an easy thing to accomplish, but as I said at the beginning, I rarely do things because they are easy – I do them because I believe in them.

It is also important to recognise that it isn't always men who discriminate against women. We are often our own worst enemies and I am often horrified by how some women fail to back their fellow women – or even actively disrupt them.

So what would be your advice to women hoping to advance in their career?

Be clear in your objectives, but be flexible in the route to them. Don't look at other women (or men) and think they have it sussed. Chances are they are feeling as insecure as you are – they just don't look it (you look the same way to them!)

Make sure if you have children, that you have the support structures at home so you are not crushed by the emotional intensity of home life and the stress of work. DO NOT FEEL GUILTY that you work and DO NOT LET ANYONE ELSE make you feel guilty. This includes your children and especially your partner, if there is one. Seeing their mothers pursuing their ambitions and contributing to the workplace gives children a great instruction.

I have often been asked if my children like me working. My response is, "No, but they don't like going to school either, switching off the xbox, eating their greens, going to bed when when they should, brushing their teeth or washing their hands," so I am often considered about my children's 'bah humbug' approach to my career.

One more piece of advice: find an unemotional mentor or sponsor who you can talk to and who will lift you when you need it (male or female, in or out of the industry).

What, for you, are the obstacles and prejudices that you might encounter as a working woman?

The biggest obstacles for working women are pay package and promotion.

It is incredible we still haven't universally fixed this.

In the USA, women get 78 per cent of what a man earns for the same role. The stats in relation to this across the globe are unending and alarming.

Many women still believe that if they stand up for themselves, it will backfire on them. What are your thoughts?

There is a truth in that, but what, as women, we don't appreciate is that it often backfires for men also. They just don't take it to heart the way we do. What we would often describe as bullying, most men accept as a matter of course and wouldn't analyse it in the way we do; they just move on.

This is one of the key issues for gender parity. The corporate model is designed for masculine behaviour. (For clarity, masculine behaviour is not exclusive to men but is predominately observed in men). Most women aren't – or do not want to be – masculine in order to get ahead, so we are looking to change the foundation of corporate behaviour to welcome more feminised behaviour, which doesn't happen overnight. (For clarity, feminised behaviour is not exclusive to women but is predominately observed in women.)

Motherhood – and maternity leave etc – can throw a spanner in the works, though. Do you think employers still hesitate to hire women because of this?

For me, it is the crux of my objective in getting involved in the woman's agenda. Unless we change the attitude and behaviour around motherhood and maternity, this is just a talking shop and it is a nettle I very rarely see grasped.

In discussing a fruitful and fulfilling career for women, we have to acknowledge that the years during which one defines and optimises their future success on the career timeline are in the thirties and forties. These years also coincide with when most women choose to tend to their biological clock because it has a finite tick. There is also a correlation between this time and the point at which the gender pay gap widens for women.

So the question for me, is how do we reframe women's careers so they can still participate in one of the most defining features of many humans' lives, that of being a parent, and still be a confident and valuable resource to the workplace and fulfil their own ambitions?

When women leave tech/telecoms for the corridors of motherhood, it is widely accepted that they can't take too long out or they are no longer current or relevant to the industry. If they do return, they invariably have to do a full-time job on a part-time package. There is no such thing as a part-time job – just a full-time job condensed into half the time for less pay, so we are penalised for efficiency. The anecdotal evidence of women being passed over for promotion at that point is striking.

If we can address this, and see parenthood as an asset on a CV, I believe the workplace will become richer for the workforce that is attracted back.

What differences exist for the younger generation and their opportunities for the future?

I think this debate will make a difference. The suffragette movement was in place for a very long time before women got the vote. I also have a firmly held view that one of the most substantial changes that will affect the next generation is fathers being more pro-active, positive and confident as parents.

I know it sounds like an odd correlation, but we teach our children through our example, and in my home our children see my husband responsible for the house as much as I am, and me being as much responsible for the family bills as he is. This is what parity is – a balance not just of gender, but of responsibilities and breaking down the received wisdom of the last generation.

To be clear, we don't have it completely right in our home life, but we strive for it!

Ireland seems to be a very progressive country – open to and supportive of parity/equal opportunities. Would you agree with this?

It is and per capita, it has a great representation but similar problems exist as elsewhere in the world. However, I think Irish women are incredibly industrious and whilst sexism is rife, the Irish women in industry that I know never let it taint their ambition for success.

Have you noticed a big difference in attitude between different countries and cultures on this topic?

Not really. It seems to be the same in Asia, Europe, Africa... everywhere. Women are desperately under-represented at all levels, but especially decision-making ones. They are terrified of the motherhood/maternity discussion because it weakens their position.

8 MOVING TO THE UPPER LEVEL: ACCEPTING – AND ACTING ON – YOUR NEXT CHALLENGES

"When one door of happiness closes, another opens; but often we look so long at the closed door that we do not see the one which has opened for us."

- Helen Keller

Actions speak louder than words... remember that saying? It is one of my inherent beliefs!

A final round-up – and then ... action. Clarity and focus, transformed into actions, are the keys to reaching your upper level.

Tick off each question:

- Do you know what you want?

- Have you got it clear?

- Where are you going?

- How are you getting there?

Really focus on these questions – and their answers – to be sure you have your objectives clear. And do you have a plan? If you don't have a plan, why not? You definitely need one.

Now you are at the stage of taking the decisions you've already made and putting them into practice, so your objectives need to be crystal clear. You need to have them written down. I always say 'written down' but also make a dream board. Instead of calling it a dream board, use it as an objective and strategy planning board and fill it with pictures to signify your objectives and motivate your progress.

I am sure you now have loads and loads of paper where you have listed all your findings, objectives, plans and actions – change this, and start using a mind map. If you're not a mind map person, go now and learn how to use one because these are much more useful. They increase your creativity and keep your motivation up. Put all your objectives on that. *(I use iMindMap by Think Buzan)*

Then, on your strategy board, attach a picture that represents each objective. Put images on the board for your step-by-step plan. Have a date for your actions. If you want to do something by the summer, have a picture of the sun or a summer scene pinned next to what you are going to do.

Try and make everything as specific as possible – but also as visual as possible, because when you visualise something, psychologically it increases your determination and innovation to achieve the desired result. When you have just a list of words on a piece of paper, without visualising it in your head, it is easy to forget or overlook part of it. But an image stays in your brain – it's just the way your brain works.

You do need a very specific plan, but don't be fixated on following it to the letter. Be prepared to move from it; jump a step (or three), go sideways, backwards or try a different route to getting there. Don't get hung up that you've missed one step. It doesn't matter. Enjoy the way you progress; enjoy the movement and the direction you follow from one part of the plan to another.

It is beneficial to factor into your plan where you'll be in three years, five years, ten years ... who you're going to be with, what you're going to be doing; even what you look like, your feelings...

Exercise 7: Visualisation Exercise

Something that helps you achieve what you want is a visualisation exercise of where you really see yourself in three years' time. Paint a vivid image in your head, see it happening through your eyes and visualise yourself in three years.

Where are you? Are you standing on the stage in front of people, presenting to a symposium? If that's your image, what are you wearing? What does your hair look like? What shoes do you have on? What have you got with you? What is in your hands? What are the objects that you're using as part of the presentation? Really see it.

Who is around you? What are they doing? What expressions are on their faces? What questions are they asking you?

And, very importantly, how do you feel? Are you feeling confident? Are you feeling happy? Are you feeling successful? Are you feeling that you're getting a good reaction from the people around you? Then think: why do you need to do this visualisation?

I'll tell you. You need it because if you're seeing and feeling that, you're already familiar with it. This makes your whole brain project into that feeling so you don't get distracted as easily. Your brain thinks you're already there. And when your brain thinks you're already doing something, it facilitates getting there more quickly.

So you need to do that for three years' time and then again for five years' time. Really think of the progress that you're going to be feeling; the progress you've made. What has changed in the scenario of where you are two years later? Then do it again for ten years. Ten years is a long time so it's difficult to be as specific. But for three years, you really can imagine it vividly.

When you've completed the plan, when you've done the visualisation of the three, five and ten years' worth of who you are, who you're with, what you're doing etc, think – what are you feeling now? Does this give you a warm, happy feeling? What does this mean to you? Do you feel energised by it?

At this stage, make any final adjustments. So, if you are feeling warm – and I don't mean a little sweet, sickly, warm, fuzzy feeling, but a real feeling of internal satisfaction that yes, I am meant to do this; this is me – then that's good. That creates energy. It gives you motivation and the dynamism that will help you get there. That, basically, is you. You've stepped into your real character, your real being.

If you don't quite have that feeling, go back a couple of steps and see what you can adjust. If what you want to do is drastically different from the situation you're in today, then you may need to make the changes slowly.

Don't try and force yourself too fast. They say Rome wasn't built in a day. It's step by step. Don't put pressure on yourself to do something too quickly; it's important to enjoy what you're doing and to feel happy with it. Yes, you have to step outside your comfort zone, but you also have to like what you're doing as well.

So, now that you have your objectives, you have your plan, you have visualised yourself in three, five and maybe even 10 years. Make a contract with yourself to enjoy every step along the way for the pleasure of doing it – NOT just for the end goal. Now accept your new future – own it. Accept the potential impact your actions have – physically, psychologically, emotionally. Mentally move forward and take the responsibility of your choice and do it. ACT! Don't dither or put off; don't think, "Well, I will..." Think "Now I am..."

What can you do immediately to start experiencing your objectives?

Firstly, have a look around you and see what you have that can be re-purposed and that fits in with your objectives. At work, see what you can do or what is available that leads in the right direction.

For example, if one of the things that you're particularly interested in is travel, start doing more work with the international department or take responsibility for international contact. Become the boss of that sector or be involved in organisation of – and going to – international meetings, contacting overseas clients, etc...

Evaluate what opportunities are already there because generally, there are many possibilities at your fingertips. They aren't necessarily new developments within your business but because you haven't had this clarity of focus before, you just haven't seen they are available.

A strange phenomenon is that when you know what you want and where you're going, opportunities will appear all around you. It's like when you decide to buy a new car. Say you decide that you want to buy a snazzy new sports mini. Your focus is lasered in, so going down the street you're going to be looking out for the sports mini. And suddenly, they pop up all over the place. Why? Because you are looking for something specific!

It is the same for work. Now you have the focus and clarity for what you want to do, you will see the opportunities that are already around you. As a first step, start by moving towards your objectives by using what you already have at work.

Next, talk to the people in your entourage because many of them will have connections in the fields you are seeking. You don't know everything about everyone. Most connections that we need – or that help us get somewhere – are no more than six steps away from where we already are, because there are so many people and activities involved in everyone's life.

Ask around. See who has a contact or some kind of involvement with what you want to do. It's always best to try with what you've got at your fingertips before you go deeper or further away.

Can working with the boss help get you into the right circle?

If your boss has a particular interest or project, it could be politic to become involved. It is always useful to have backing so if you really want promotion to a certain position, and you need to get the boss to support you, find out what his/her interests are. Find out in what way they could link up with your own objectives.

Quite often, you'll know this already if you are working closely with him/her. If not, you may know someone – or you might have a good relationship with someone – who is currently working closely with the boss. Once you have the necessary information, try and create an opportunity for doing work on this project and make appropriate and productive suggestions to show your interest – and your talent. Think of ways – that the boss will appreciate – in which you can improve the productivity of the project and/or department, particularly with issues relating to the direction in which you want to move.

Basically, think of this move as a marketing plan. Approach it as though you have a new project or a new product which you want to promote to a new market. You are the product; the boss is the market...

How would you promote it? How would you want him/her to see it? How would you seduce the market to present maximum appeal? Then start pushing that to maximum effect.

What supporting arguments can you use to create positive reaction in company hierarchy about why women – and particularly you – are a good choice as a senior executive at board level?

Don't hesitate to use the statistics which prove that if you've got a woman on the board, the company has better financial results and less risk. Financially, having a woman (or women) on the board is better for the company. The risk levels are amortised.

As well as statistics, focus on how feminine skills are different to male ones. Draw attention to the success women have in negotiation: women are much less conflictual than men, so frequently they get a better deal and have very good results.

Therefore, you can underline how it is good to have a woman's objectivity at board level because if you have an all-male board, they obviously will think like men. Much of the objectivity that is necessary for very senior decisions and responsibility is not naturally included when there is an all-male viewpoint. The feminine strengths and different focus give good balance and raise new options – as well as another vision on risk assessment and ways of development.

So you present your skills to show the chairman/CEO that you are a bonus because you see an angle that isn't immediately visible to other members of the board. Therefore, you are helping them achieve a more rounded view of everything that could happen.

Supporting equality and equal opportunities by supporting the right kind of women's career advancement in companies and industries.

This can be a very sensitive issue because not only do we have the challenge of men versus women on gender, balance, equality, etc, but the aspect of dedication and acting for the right reasons also has to be considered. Unfortunately, there are some people who try to take advantage; they're not truly committed to doing the necessary work or taking the necessary responsibility in all walks of life – this can be true of either gender, and in all kinds of professional situations. It is unfortunate, though, when fighting to improve conditions, get recognition and/or acceptance on a delicate subject.

Organising strategic events can be effective - lunches, meetings, seminars, workshops... They don't necessarily need to be external events; you can organise them in-house yourself, so that you can talk about men and women working together. You can include subjects like opportunities for promotion, responsibilities, different skillsets and much more.

You can create an action group for women to discuss the potential problems affecting them in the workplace, how to act and react, what they can focus on to improve the opportunities and different skills – eg negotiation, discussions, presentations, public speaking – and how to be successful in these areas. You also need to help women become aware of what their choices really are, and help them see and understand the strengths they have so they can use them to good effect.

A lot of women don't get the necessary business skills training that men automatically receive because even in universities and business schools, there are still predeterminations, so women are not always treated equally. Show your female colleagues that if they say they want to do something, they should follow through. They need to be responsible for their own future and show integrity in their pursuit of this.

Make sure the training opportunities are there, and there is focus on the acquisition of necessary business skills. Listen to women about what they themselves feel they need in order to get promotion in the company.

At the same time, listen to men and their view of where problems lie. By bringing everything out into the open and having a full understanding of both sides of every aspect, you can then prove the strong points of women. You must not overlook the importance of these in complementing the strong points of men – the aim is not to produce reverse discrimination. We are not trying to have women ruling the world – at least not yet! – we are simply looking for equal opportunities, treatment and respect.

If a person is capable, they should be chosen on aptitude – irrespective of whether they are a man or a woman. You as a woman obviously want to get that position; you want that promotion. Therefore, you need to focus on acquiring the skills, the strengths, the abilities that you *haven't* been given before. You need to open the door on what has been lacking in your career to help the women, who are still a little further down the ladder, to have the opportunity of taking those places.

"One of the most courageous things you can do is identify yourself, know who you are, what you believe in and where you want to go."

- Sheila Murray Bethel

May I introduce Gabriele, an inspiring role model for us all. Gabi is a warm, caring leader and a very capable businesswoman. Her insight and experience, along with her supportive leadership, have helped many women up their career ladder. Listen to some of the highlights and choices she has made during her career...

 ## EXCEPTIONAL WOMEN: Success Talks

An interview with: Gabi Zedlmayer

VP and Chief Progress Officer at HP, member of the board of directors of Hewlett-Packard GmbH, Germany. President of the Women's Council of HypoVereinsbank UNICREDIT, member of the EU Commission e-skills leadership board, the Computer Science Advisory Board of the University of People, and Junior Achievement Europe, Middle East and Africa (EMEA), the World Economic Forum's Council on Social Innovation and the Corporate Advisory Group of the We Mean Business Coalition.

Honoured by Newsweek and the Daily Beast in 2011 as one of 150 "women who shake the world". In 2012 named by FastCompany as a member of the League of Extraordinary Women, awarded the DLDWomen Impact Award. In February 2015, InspiringFifty named her as one of the 50 most inspiring women in technology.

What is the first thing that comes to mind when you hear about women's freedom to choose what they really want to do?

It's not that simple – if they want a family and a top level career, they need a supportive partner. Then they really have a choice.

List three pieces of advice you have on obtaining career fulfilment.

- Take charge of your career

- Be confident in your abilities and market them appropriately

- Ask for support and be persistent here

What are three mistakes people make about career objectives?

- They don't take the time to continuously invest in themselves

- They don't articulate their objectives to the appropriate senior executives

- They don't look push for alternatives if being overlooked for the xxxth time

What are some actionable takeaways you would like to leave women about change and choosing what is right for them?

- Figure out what you really want and what it takes to get there

- Be persistent in obtaining those goals and don't give up too easily

- Get help from sponsors

Why is career fulfilment important?

- It's a large part of our life
- It surely influences our private life to a large degree as well (including health etc)
- It's an opportunity to make a difference

You have an amazing and very impressive career, starting more than 20 years ago. You have held many different positions. Can you sum up the high points?

There have been lots of those! Following two exciting years at Eastern Airlines in the software automation department, I joined a start-up called Compaq in Europe, Middle East and Africa. I was part of a team that created something big and meaningful – the first set of hi-powered portable PCs – and it was an outstanding experience. Growing a career in the IT industry kept on being an energising, motivating and rewarding experience. In IT, nothing ever stays the same – change has to be your middle name. There is always new stuff to learn and apply; it's just fascinating.

What inspired your choices for your career?

I was inspired by the IT industry and by the people who helped shape it at the time – and of course by my colleagues. We all shared the same spirit – "Let's get on with it". "No" was not really an option so we always looked for innovative and creative ways to get our goals accomplished. It was really the special environment and the spirit of our company that gave me the confidence and the belief in myself that was necessary to pursue my aspirations. Later on, when HP and Compaq merged, I was inspired by a terrific business executive: Debra Dunn.

She ran Corporate Affairs for HP at the time and did breakthrough work in global citizenship. I wanted to fill her shoes, and I had the opportunity to transform HP's philanthropic activities into true social innovation initiatives that are creating shared value.

What obstacles did you have to overcome at the beginning of your career, and how did you achieve this?

There have been times when I felt that I should have advanced to the next level when actually, somebody else did. Usually – or let me correct that - it was *always* a man. But I did not let that break my spirit – I kept pursuing my strategy and plans, always keeping true to my values and what is important to me. I also looked for projects that were above and beyond the scope of my responsibility, in order to get some visibility. That includes volunteering opportunities and, for example, providing creative support for major meetings that made specific executives look good. It helped me build relationships and strengthen my network. A great network within the company – and externally of course as well – is worth a lot.

Why do you think there is an image of women in tech having problems being accepted/recognised for their true worth? Did you experience it?

The pipeline issue probably starts in kindergarten. I think it is fair to say that we often don't appreciate children's talents and don't further their interests. Most big mathematicians are also great musicians, but music is not a subject that is considered important when we teach our children; maths and sciences are considered important! But the way we teach them is not interesting and meaningful to children – and especially girls. If we started to create hands-on science experiences for girls that show them how maths, physics and chemistry are all important in creating fashion or music, or help save our environment in the future, we would have a lot more interested kids and we could start building a pipeline of STEM talent.

We need to start early on and then ensure that women advance through the organisations as men do. In the future, this will be easier, in my opinion, since organisation structures will become more fluid; the workplaces as we have known them will not continue to exist longer term, and those who invest in themselves and their careers will excel.

It is not easy to have a good balance between personal and professional life. How do you manage it with all your responsibilities?

I get up before 5am and run for 90 minutes every day. It clears my head, keeps me fit and puts me in a great mood. Otherwise, I have a great husband who helps manage everything!

How do you handle the pressure? What do you do to de-stress?

Again, running every day helps tremendously. And also, I tend to put things more into perspective these days than I did twenty years ago. Works well!

It is often said that being organised is the key to success. What does your typical day look like?

I travel a lot, and lots of unexpected stuff happens when you are travelling in Africa, India or Central America – or in Europe or the US for that matter. But technology helps tremendously in keeping to the schedule – with ubiquitous access anywhere, anytime, you can make any airport your office and that usually works for me.

What differences exist for the younger generation and its opportunities for the future?

It is a whole new world out there. Our parents' job markets no longer exist. It is about investing in yourself throughout your life, and reinventing yourself and your job on an ongoing basis.

You are strongly involved in several boards and forums, so you necessarily have a long-term vision. What changes in companies/mentalities do you expect?

Much more crowdsourcing of ideas – degrees won't matter as much when you are looking for a job – few fixed contracts, lots of freelance project work, new business models every day. All exciting but people need to stay on top of what is happening.

Have you noticed a big difference in the attitude towards gender balance/parity between the different countries and cultures that you work with?

For sure. There are huge differences between the different countries I have visited. The great opportunity I see here is that we can learn from those societies that have more women engineers, more female leaders, more board members and more gender balance in general. With today's communication opportunities, we have no excuses not to get a better understanding of why some countries are ahead – and how some of these successes can be potentially adapted and transferred. Live and learn.

"Don't limit yourself.
Many people limit themselves to what they think they
can do. You can go as far as your mind lets you.
What you believe, remember you can achieve."

- Mary Kay Ash

9 YOUR CAREER, YOUR LIFE, YOUR CHOICE – AT ANY AGE!

"The question isn't who is going to let me;
it's who is going to stop me."

- Ayn Rand (Novelist/Philosopher)

Just because you have hit forty five doesn't mean that you have to wind down your career, that you have reached your limit, that you can't completely change direction, start your own business or generally do anything new, different and challenging that you want to do – far from it!

Think of my favourite 'glass ceiling grans': Christine Lagarde, Hillary Clinton, Marillyn Hewson (Lockheed Martin), Indra Nooyi (Pepsi), Carolyn McCall (EasyJet) and Moya Greene (Royal Mail) – what do these leaders have in common? Power – obviously – but also being women and over fifty! Winners on two strikes: one in the eye for chauvinists and equally – or more importantly – ageists!

So what could be the reasons why they are really stepping into the high point of their careers now? The answer is age plus experience. They are the granny age. It is a time of life when many – both men and women – are starting to think of retirement: gardening, relaxation, winding down in general. But it doesn't have to be like that. For these shining examples of energy, dynamism, ability and ambition have had their families; mostly their children are at – or have left – university, business school etc. These powerful women have managed their lives and careers around their families, which has given them an opportunity to mature, gain extensive experience and understand more deeply the challenges of leading, managing and delegating.

They are now coming into their own and have the time, energy and availability to ramp up their careers and lead. They have had more education than any women before them, and in several ways they are better suited to change gears now and take power later in life. Whether it is fair or not, many women are held back until mid-life by motherhood and having to be more present in the home. Now, at this stage, they have already proved themselves during the previous ten to twenty years and this leads to a new possibility: they can have it all by having it at different times. It is not uncommon for relatively high-level female executives to hover in the sidelines until their children get to university age, when they can then move into overdrive with at least fifteen years ahead of them to break right through that glass ceiling.

And it doesn't only happen in politics and business. Now, models are also being valued and becoming the 'égérie' of some fashion and beauty houses. Think of Helen Mirren, 70, for L'Oréal; Marie Helvin, 62, for lingerie by Aliza Reger.

Overall, it is a pleasure to see how opportunities are opening up for us 50+ers who enjoy life and don't consider ourselves any older than we were twenty years ago – just wiser, more experienced and better suited to set an excellent example and lead with focus, support and understanding.

We also have the experience and know-how to 're-purpose' our skills and open up new opportunities in different directions. Are you suited to passing on your talents by mentoring in your own (or other) businesses or corporations? More and more businesses and individuals are looking for mentors to help transitions and support newly promoted executives. Not only does it give you a chance to remodel your expertise, but also you are helping someone moving up. Helping others has its own reward. Also, it is fun to be working with younger people, who are full of enthusiasm and new ideas. You can create an amazing team!

If your current job seems to be winding down and you suspect your company no longer looks on you as a rising star or high flyer, look to ALL your skills and interests. Think about what you do – or are involved in – outside of work. Consider what your long-put-aside passions and dreams are and see how you can resurrect them. Analyse all this as you would a new contract in project management. Go through a personal SWOT, look at the hedgehog concept, check out the TOWS matrix, use the process I created – SCOPE for Career Fulfilment – and with all these tools, see how you can realign strengths and choices, then create your strategy for changing direction to open up new opportunities and, as an added value, gain more fulfilment in your life and career.

They say a change is as good as a rest, and boy is that true. You would be amazed at how full of energy you are each morning as you wake up with additional purpose and focus; how you jump out of bed looking forward to what the day will bring. You look younger, feel better, have a smile on your face and why not? You have discovered your own personal 'Fountain of Youth'.

What is it that makes so many silver goddesses want to continue working extensively at quite a late time of their life? We only have to look at my favourite actresses who give us just as much of a good example as all the high-flying business leaders for responsibility, dedication and hard work.

My favourite actresses are Judi Dench and Maggie Smith – both over eighty – along with Helen Mirren, a mere spring chicken at seventy.

All of them are fabulous, active, much in demand and obviously love life, so what is their secret and how do they keep it? I think the words 'love life' give us a clue.

They all keep working at their age and show no signs of stopping. So, why do they do it? It's not for the money; it's not for the fame – they obviously have as much of both as they want. It is for the love of their art – they do what they love and they love what they do.

Not only that – they know who they are. They are down to earth, direct, no-nonsense and don't have airy-fairy illusions. If they like – or don't like – something, they have no hesitation in speaking up. They are comfortable with themselves; happy in their own skins. Not for them all the panic-stricken thoughts of plastic surgery, botox, nips and tucks or any of the other 'aesthetic procedures' that some may consider. They carry their grey hair and wrinkles as part of their natural charm and balanced love of life.

Where do they find the energy? Not only are they still appearing in blockbusters, but also on the stage. Both filming and performing on stage are known for their gruelling schedules, long hours and pressure but again, these remarkable women know themselves well. They know and love their craft, and as we know from our own daily lives, passion fuels energy. When we are doing something we truly love, we have endless energy and we will organise our day to best generate more time and energy for our passions.

We can be as active and dynamic as we choose to be

These actresses also show us how ageing is 'cool', and that we can be as active and dynamic as we choose to be. Just think of some of the films that have come out recently, such as 'Best Exotic Marigold Hotel', all about how you manage ageing and longevity. A few years ago, no film financiers or distributors would have touched it; they would not have imagined for one moment that it could be an interesting subject – let alone a hit – but it earned over $135 million worldwide. The second 'Best Exotic Marigold Hotel' film added to its already fabulous cast by including big screen heartthrob, Richard Gere, aged sixty-five.

People's previous negative views on ageing are changing. We can see for ourselves that we now have the opportunity to enjoy our life and take – or create – more time for our own dynamic, fun and fulfilling lifestyle as much as these three great Dames. Put more focus on your passions and interests, incorporate more of them into your daily life and see your energy, satisfaction and quality of life levels take off.

Do what you love and love what you do!

"Time and trouble will tame an advanced young woman, but an advanced old woman is uncontrollable by any earthly force."

\- Dorothy L. Sayers

I am delighted to introduce you to Ceri, a trailblazer and true expert in all matters relating to careers and ageing with zing!

 ## ASK the EXPERT:

Ceri Wheeldon

Nearly 30 years' experience working on strategic headhunting assignments in UK, North America and across Europe. Expert on issues facing the 50plus jobseeker. Frequently featured in UK media on this topic. Founder of **_FabafterFifty.co.uk_**, a resource site to help women over 50 live life to the full...

What is the first thing that comes to mind when you hear about women's freedom to choose what they really want to do?

I think that for many generations, women had their lives mapped out for them, or even felt pressured to meet the expectations of others – both society and family. But times have changed. Traditional roles have changed.

We do have the opportunity to do what we really want– providing we have the courage and confidence to stand up and choose. But first, we need to know what it is we really want to do. We have more choice, but we also need to be more decisive.

Can you briefly explain why ageing – and being older – is such a liberating and productive time of life?

I believe we can benefit from the experience we have gained in so many walks of life and bring them together – we are experts in multi-tasking and communicating across the generations. We have made many mistakes and hopefully learned from them, growing as a result. We can bring all of our skills and wisdom together and set our goals and expectations. We have nothing to prove to anyone but ourselves. We are comfortable in our own skins, know ourselves and what drives us in our lives and careers. We are able to focus on what really matters and set our own goals.

Why is ageing viewed so negatively in so many Western cultures, when in many others it is honoured and revered?

We do seem to be living in an age-obsessed culture where the superficial is appreciated more than substance! We are surrounded by images of youth in the media, implying that youth is to be aspired to. Even our daily beauty regime is conducted with products prefaced by 'anti-ageing' – as though ageing is something to be avoided at all costs.

In other cultures, multi-generational families live closer together, and the young appreciate the life experience of the older generation, who in turn have an active role in the daily lives of the younger. In our culture, this happens much less often. Families are more fragmented. We hide our older generation away. We lose their wit and wisdom, while those in care homes lose the contact with the younger generation that help keep them connected, positive and wanting to share. We have too few activities across the generations where young and old can really appreciate each other.

What are three mistakes people – and companies – make about ageing and older employees, whatever their level, due to this negativity?

1. The assumption that older workers are 'winding down' and not open to learning new things. You need to stress at any interview or in work situations that you are open to doing new things. Demonstrate that you have taken courses or taken up new interests in your own time, and put your name forward for any new training opportunities in your workplace. Demonstrate high energy levels. Stay current - show that you are up to date with the latest technology. Also, dress for today – not two decades ago; impressions do count.

2. Older workers are more difficult to manage. Research by the University of Philadelphia showed that younger managers were reluctant to hire older workers as they weren't sure how to manage them. On one hand, this is a training issue that needs to be addressed by employers, but we can also make sure that at interviews, we show that we can be easy to manage. Ask how objectives are set and performance measured. Ensure that you stress that you enjoy working with – and learning from – younger colleagues (and bosses). Do not come across as someone who has nothing more to learn, or who would find it difficult to take direction.

3. Older workers have no ambition. With many working until the age of seventy, you have far too many years ahead of you to simply tread water. Emphasise what you have achieved in the past fifteen years...and what you plan to achieve in the next fifteen!

What are some actionable takeaways you would like to leave women about change and choosing what is right for them, particularly as they age?

If you do choose to change careers, make sure there really is a market for what you want to do, and that you have the right skills – or can acquire them at a cost and within a timeframe that is viable. Make sure that what you choose to do in the future can meet your financial needs. Do your research up front.

I had a situation where someone in her fifties came to me, incredibly disheartened having given up her job and taken a two-year course to become a natural beauty therapist. She needed to make £60k a year to meet her needs. She had not found employment and believed her age was against her. In fact, there were a number of issues, and in this person's case it wasn't her age. Out of a class of thirty - of all ages - only three had found full-time employment....and none of them at anywhere near the £60k level she needed.

What she wanted/needed to earn and what the market was prepared to pay were vastly different. She did not do her research beforehand. Nor had she factored in the cost of supporting herself for two years when enrolling in the course. None of the potential employers she applied to for jobs had even heard of the school, and so did not recognise her new qualification. She had tried to find private clients, but her marketing was mainly via twitter, which resulted in connections all over the world – but not locally with people who would ever be paying customers.

You really do need to look at all the aspects. Follow your dream, but be realistic. Ensure there is a market, and that you are realistic about the timescales and costs involved. It is more difficult to recover financially from a wrong two-year investment in our fifties or sixties than it is in our twenties. Do your homework, make the right decisions and you will love the changes you make.

Why is it so important to find ways to be fulfilled in life and your career?

I believe that in order to live life to the full, it is important to set new challenges in different areas of your life to stay interested and engaged, and which are also interesting to others.

Achievements, large and small, deliver greater self-confidence and make you more enthusiastic about life in general – whether it's signing that big deal or trying a new recipe for a family occasion.

It is about balance, and work is not everything so you need to invest in friendships, relationships and outside interests too.

When you stand still for too long, you stop living! You don't want to look back on life and think 'If only I had tried x.....'

EPILOGUE –
HEALTHY MIND, HEALTHY BODY!

Mindset and the whole mind-body experience – mental, physical and emotional – for optimal results, fulfilment and success...

'To keep the body in good health is a duty... otherwise we shall not be able to keep our mind strong and clear.'
- Buddha

To reiterate, and I cannot underline strongly enough:

For the deepest fulfilment we need to welcome the value of the whole mind-body experience. When every aspect is in harmony and flow, the greatest success and happiness are obtained. Therefore, healthy mind = healthy body! Incorporating all areas – mental, physical and emotional – will give you the optimum results for fulfilment and success.

This means if we include health, fitness and mind-set as being integral parts of the whole, we have a far greater capacity for achieving our objectives – freedom and fulfilment! Just for the moment, start mulling these over in your head. How much focus do you put on the following as integral parts of your fulfilment and success?

Healthy eating:

- Avoiding fast food, junk, salt, sugar, pre-prepared, processed, salamis, pâtés, cold cuts etc, animal fats, most meat and dairy...

- Favouring natural fresh, organic fruit, vegetables, leaves, salads, seeds, some fish, minimal quantities of organically raised meat if you absolutely must.

Exercise:

- Regular activity of your choice that incorporates stretching/flexibility, strength training and cardio. My favourites are dancing, walking, Pilates, yoga, T'ai Chi.

- Getting out in the sun and fresh air every day – try a daily thirty-minute walk outside (building up to longer over time), preferably in nature and the countryside but failing that, in a local park or beside a canal.

Mental/emotional relaxation:

- Meditation - or if you are uncomfortable with the idea of this, just a regular quiet time each day, when you disconnect from the unavoidable stresses and strains of daily life.

- Avoiding letting yourself react negatively in stressful situations

- Focusing on your achievements: the small as much as the large ones

- Keeping positive thoughts, positive action and what you get pleasure from foremost in your mind.

- Enjoying all the moments in the day (not always fixating on goals) so to use a well-known but very accurate cliché - enjoy the journey, not just the destination!

> *'The purpose of our lives is to be happy.'*
> - Dalai Lama

YOU CAN LEARN MORE ABOUT OUR WONDERFUL EXPERTS AND INTERVIEWEES

- **Mariela Dabbah:**

  www.marieladabbah.com

  www.redshoemovement.com

  linkedin.com/in/marieladabbah

- **John P Strelecky:**

  www.johnpstrelecky.com

  www.bigfiveforlife.com

  www.whycafe.com

  linkedin.com/in/johnstrelecky

- **Jo-Ann A Hamilton:**

  www.secretbirdslondon.com

  linkedin.com/in/jo-ann-a-hamilton-69475225

- **Ceri Wheeldon:**

  www.fabafterfifty.co.uk

  uk.linkedin.com/in/ceri-wheeldon-8b7153

- **Louise O'Sullivan:**

  uk.linkedin.com/in/louise-o-sullivan-81054244

- **Stina Ehrensvard:**

  linkedin.com/in/stinaehrensvard

- **Ruth Sacks:**

  uk.linkedin.com/in/ruthsacks

- **Gabriele Zedlmayer:**

  de.linkedin.com/in/gabriele-zedlmayer-84a24a2

RESOURCES:

You can access all the resources and downloads associated with the book here:

http://unstoppablegoddess.life/book-resources/

As a thank you for purchasing this book, we would like to offer you one month's free membership of the Unstoppable Goddess Experience, and an extra special gift when you participate in the Unstoppable Goddess Elite - Bermuda Breakthrough Mastermind and Retreat.

Visit www.WomenUP.global for more information about our philosophy, the *SCOPE Process for Career Fulfilment* and the *Unstoppable Goddess 4-dimensional Life Design* as well as information about groups, events and training collection, including the exclusive 'Unstoppable Goddess Elite - Bermuda Breakthrough Mastermind and Retreat.'

NEWS AND EVENTS

In the pipeline, my next books:

- **Glass Ceiling Grans:** the Silver Goddess Experience – The woman's guide to a fun, fulfilling and dynamic career at 50+

- **The Entrepreneurial Goddess** – The woman's guide to creating, managing and enjoying your own successful business.

- **The Unstoppable Goddess 4 - dimensional Life Design** – Success as a slim, fit, happy and fulfilled woman - at every level!

New and exciting opportunity:

Sign up now to receive the news first, on opening day, for information and registrations:

<u>**The Unstoppable Goddess Elite**</u>
<u>**Bermuda Breakthrough Mastermind & Retreat**</u>

ABOUT THE AUTHOR

Anna Letitia Cook is a speaker, consultant and mentor for women's entrepreneurship and transitions, career fulfilment and success, 50+ career rejuvenation and renewal.

Passionate about mentoring women to find clarity and fulfilment in their choices, she created and became CEO of her first company in the entertainment industry at age thirty-two.

Midlife approaching, and hungry for a dynamic change, she refocused her experience, founding WomenUP Ltd to help women shape their own future. She is the creator of the *Unstoppable Goddess 4-dimensional Life Design* and the *SCOPE Process for Career Fulfilment.*

Anna started her career in the City [of London]. She worked primarily in press, shipping and oil before moving into entertainment and then investment/real estate. During that time she worked in many different countries, spending several years in Bermuda, Spain and France, so was able to experience first-hand how to integrate with many different cultures, mentalities and ways of working.

She founded WomenUP Ltd as an answer from the many conversations had with clients—CEOs, directors and senior managers—as finding clarity and fulfilment in your career choices is not always easy in this day and age with all the pressure on achieving a traditional, male dominated vision of success!

A radio show host and regular feature and editorial writer in several online magazines, Anna has weekly columns focused on helping women and the 50+ sector enjoy and energise both their personal and professional life.

Designated as one of UN Women's 2016-2017 Global Champions for Change @ Empower Women.

<u>www.womenup.global/meet-anna/</u>